Functional Family Therapy

FUNCTIONAL FAMILY THERAPY

James Alexander
University of Utah

Bruce V. Parsons
Family Therapy Institute of Laguna Beach

Brooks/Cole Publishing Company
Monterey, California

Brooks/Cole Publishing Company
A Division of Wadsworth, Inc.

Printed in the United States of America

10 9 8 7 6 5 4 3 2 1

Library of Congress Cataloging in Publication Data

Alexander, James, 1941--
    Functional family therapy.

    Includes bibliographies and index.
    1. Family psychotherapy. I. Parsons, Bruce V.,
(date). II. Title.
RC488.5.A43   616.89'156   81-17058
ISBN 0-8185-0485-4   AACR2

    Subject Editor: *Claire Verduin*
    Manuscript Editor: *Pam Fischer*
    Production Editor: *John Bergez*
    Interior Design: *Angela Lee*
    Cover Design: *Kath Minerva*
    Illustrations: *Kathleen Kusy*
    Typesetting: *Linda Andrews, Ashland, Oregon*

Preface

For decades following Alfred Adler's pioneering work in the 1920s, family therapy enjoyed only a minor or adjunct role among the various treatment approaches in the field of mental health. Recently, however, family therapy has experienced phenomenal growth in impact and popularity. The functional family therapy approach described in this book, a synthesis of interpersonal, behavioral, and systems orientations, represents a new evolutionary step in the treatment of families. It is based on the substantial works of our predecessors and the experience derived from many hours of seeing families in both clinical and research contexts.

The goal of this book is to provide a clear description of the procedures and structure necessary for the successful practice of family therapy. Family therapists need an unambiguous conceptual framework and a set of specific techniques for dealing with families in distress. At the same time, however, they cannot succeed if they are merely technicians. For this reason the book is also designed to enhance the flexibility and creativity therapists need to respond effectively to the myriad needs, idiosyncrasies, and forms of resistance presented by the different families they see.

To this end much of the material in the book is presented in a somewhat intuitive manner, often by example and analogy. Part One describes the functional family model as it generally applies to *all* families, including the specific conceptual, technical, and interpersonal skills required of all family therapists. *Conceptual skills* (Chapter 1) comprise the perspectives therapists need to understand families, as well as the knowledge necessary for developing appropriate therapeutic goals and selecting suitable techniques. *Technical skills* (Chapters 2, 3, and 4) include the verbal, nonverbal, and physical tools that therapists use as vehicles of change. They represent the technology of what therapists do, based on their conceptual understanding of what needs to be done. *Interpersonal skills* (Chapter 5) represent the *way* therapists apply their techniques. The efficacy of the techniques depends significantly on the atmosphere and family attitudes created through these interpersonal skills.

Part Two is designed to facilitate therapists' flexibility by describing each of the phases of intervention, with emphasis on the goals of each phase, rather than on the specific techniques (Chapter 6). Part Two also describes a number of unique developmental and structural aspects of particular families that require specific techniques (Chapter 7). Finally, the worksheets presented in the Appendixes are intended for use on each of the cases therapists encounter. They provide a monitoring function useful for understanding each family, as well as the therapist's style and its impact.

In writing this book we had an advantage not shared by our predecessors, who often had to forge ideas alone, without the help of one another's experience and knowledge. To each of them we offer our gratitude, and we urge readers to pursue the works cited in the lists of Suggested Readings.

The task of interfacing abstract theory and solid research data with the pain and joy of very real families has been arduous. The book would not accurately reflect all these elements without the contributions of the families we have treated, the colleagues and predecessors who have taught us so much through their writing and example, and the trainees who have given us feedback through their questions and performance. We are also indebted to Cole Barton, who edited several drafts, coauthored the Appendixes, and taught us much.

Several people read all or part of the manuscript and provided helpful reviews: Margaret Blake, University of Northern Colorado; Dave Capuzzi, Portland State University; Lucy Rau Ferguson, Michigan State University; Grace Seibert Larke, Syracuse University; Barry Levin, University of Missouri (Columbia); and John Vincent, University of Houston.

We add our love to the thanks we offer to our wives, Judy

Alexander and Barbara Parsons, and our children, Jayme and Molly. More than anyone else, they helped make this book happen.

James F. Alexander
Bruce V. Parsons

Contents

Functional Family Therapy

PART ONE

SKILLS FOR CHANGING FAMILIES

Families in which one or more members are poorly motivated for change are a challenge to family therapists. Such families often place heavy demands on public service agencies when they have in addition only limited resources and urgent problems that must be resolved in a short period of time. Therapists and treatment agencies can thus derive considerable benefit from knowing how to effectively treat these families.

Functional family therapy is a model for treating both difficult families and those families that are generally seen as more desirable because they have a higher level of motivation and more resources. The model is composed of the specific conceptual, technical, and interpersonal elements that research and clinical experience have shown to be both effective and efficient. Because these elements have roots in various sources, it is important to note the context in which they were developed. Prior to the classic works of such authors as Ackerman (1966), Bell (1961), Bowen (1966), Haley (1963, 1969, 1971, 1973, 1976, 1980), Hoffman (1976), Jackson (1965), Minuchin (1974), Satir (1967), and

Zuk (1978), family therapy lacked a theoretical framework and set of techniques to define it as well as to guide family therapists in their endeavors. As a result, until recently most approaches to dealing with families were based on a combination of folklore, intuition, experience, and an often awkward extension of the concepts and techniques developed for individual intrapsychic therapy.

With the development of a solid base of theory and techniques, however, family therapy has matured into a widely accepted and powerful treatment modality, as reflected in the fact that there are now more than 300 free-standing family therapy training institutes (Framo, 1979). Contributing to the widespread impact of family therapy has been the appearance of excellent reviews and edited books (for example, Gurman & Kniskern, 1978, 1980; Olson, 1970; Stanton, 1980a, 1980b) and of books and articles that provide extensions of social-learning theory into the family realm (Johnson & Christensen, 1975; Martin, 1967; Patterson, 1971; Patterson & Gullion, 1971; Patterson, McNeil, Hawkins, & Phelps, 1967; Patterson & Reid, 1970; Stuart, 1971; Stuart & Lott, 1972; Tharp & Wetzel, 1969; Weathers & Liberman, 1976), theoretical extensions from interactional and communication perspectives (Altman & Taylor, 1973; Bach & Wyden, 1970; Beier, 1966; von Bertalanffy, 1948; Carson, 1969; Lewin, 1951; Sullivan, 1947; Watzlawick, Beavin, & Jackson, 1967; Watzlawick, Weakland, & Fisch, 1974; Weakland, 1976; Weakland, Fisch, Watzlawick, & Bodin, 1974), and a strong research base for basic principles and therapeutic effectiveness (Alexander, 1973, 1974; Alexander & Barton, 1976, 1980; Alexander & Parsons, 1973; Barton & Alexander, 1977, 1980; Klein, Alexander, & Parsons, 1977; Parsons & Alexander, 1973; Stanton, 1980a, 1980b; Stanton & Todd, 1979).

Interest in family therapy has also been prompted because it is adisciplinary. Traditional training programs in mental health disciplines involve extensive time and formal certification, and until recently the delivery of therapy has generally been restricted to mental health professionals. Yet an appreciation of family problems has also been necessary for nursery school teachers, recreation therapists, public health nurses, police personnel, pediatricians, and many other professionals. As a result, family intervention has not been restricted by disciplinary or even interdisciplinary boundaries.

Further, as family therapy techniques and theories have developed, it has become clear that effective family intervention is not a simple or unimodal phenomenon. In fact, to create the conditions necessary for effective intervention therapists must be simultaneously proficient in three distinct skill categories: conceptual (how to think about families), technical (what to do with families to help them change), and interpersonal (how to apply techniques). Part One of this book discusses each of these skill classes in detail.

Conceptual skills (Chapter 1) are needed to understand the dynamics of family interaction and to know what needs to be changed. How should we think about families, what should we watch for and what should we disregard so that we at least have a chance of understanding them? Ideally, this understanding should be based on careful analysis, but most of the time it is based simply on intuition. Sometimes we know, but more often we guess. Thus, conceptual skills help us in the process of guessing as much as in ultimately arriving at an accurate understanding. Learning to become a family therapist is analogous to learning to drive a car. At first we jerkily attend to everything—often overcorrecting one process while ignoring another—with the result being at best an awkward movement in our intended direction. But after practice we learn that many tasks become automatic and can be filtered out, allowing us to focus on other important matters. Even "quiet" families present the therapist with a wealth of complex information, including their histories, subtle and not-so-subtle nonverbal cues, complex interactions with the outside world, and a mixture of attitudes, feelings, behaviors, and hopes. Learning what dimensions to select and change, as well as what to ignore, is essential if the therapist is to avoid being caught up in irresolvable complexities and led down the many garden paths characteristic of troubled families.

Beyond the issue of understanding is the problem of motivation. In contrast to many intervention models, functional family therapy is based on the belief that motivation is to a great extent the responsibility of the therapist not just the family. From this perspective, family therapists are not merely chemists or engineers with the sole responsibility of coming up with the correct drug or cure or technique. They are also practitioners who must help families use their drugs and cures and techniques. Both therapists and families must adopt the conceptual framework that best helps the families become motivated, then use this motivation to effect efficient and realistic change (Stanton, 1980b; Stanton & Todd, 1979).

Thus, in the conceptual-skill category we are talking about a conceptual orientation. Professionals who are successful with families have a distinct view, seeing the family not as harboring a patient or as being the victim of pathological behavior but as a constellation of interacting groups that behave according to certain principles and can be changed by utilizing those same principles. To teach this orientation is perhaps the most difficult task of trainers and consultants who work with family counselors. Yet without this orientation even the most technically skilled clinician will have great difficulty in initiating and maintaining the changes desired.

Technical skills (Chapters 2, 3, and 4) are the basic tools of family therapy, the moment-to-moment operations and procedures that can produce change. Much of a family therapist's effectiveness is determined by the therapist's familiarity with and ability to utilize a range of specific techniques in the appropriate circumstances. In general these techniques are designed to change four different aspects of family life: the perceptions and feelings family members have about themselves and each other; specific overt behaviors such as tantrums that constitute a problem for one or more family members; specific physiological states such as anxiety; and the communicative behaviors that create, maintain, and modify problematic perceptions, feelings, behaviors, and physiological states.

Behavior is observable, but the feelings and thoughts that accompany it must be inferred. Family members face this inference problem when they must interpret both their own behavior and the behavior of others. "Did my husband refuse sex to offend me or because he loves someone else or because he really is just tired?" The fact that inferences must be made adds enormous complexity to the therapeutic task because behavior change by itself is often unacceptable to family members in distress. All family therapists have heard such refrains as "It isn't just refusing sex, I need for him to *want* to make love to me" or "Sure, I want the garbage taken out, but that's not the real problem. The problem is he doesn't *feel* like helping out." In other words, behavior has meaning for people; they characteristically give themselves reasons for the thoughts and feelings that accompany it.

Thus while it may be maladaptive behavior that brings the family into therapy, family therapists must recognize and deal with the cognitive and affective realms of family functioning as well as the behavioral realms in order to produce lasting change. To do so therapists must possess a wide and flexible range of technical skills because, in different ways and at different times, these realms interact to facilitate positive change or to impede it. Thus, in one family a particular set of techniques may work beautifully, while in another family the same techniques may fail miserably. When therapists have the technical skills to utilize a wide range of interventions (as well as the conceptual skills to know which techniques to use in a particular circumstance), they can work with many different families and situations effectively. In the functional family model, the phases of assessment, therapy, and education are designed to deal systematically with the behavioral, cognitive, and affective realms.

Interpersonal skills (Chapter 5) have had a curious place in the therapy literature throughout the years. On the one hand some family therapists believe interpersonal skills—of one variety or another—are all therapists need to successfully help people change; therapists need only to *be* something (congruent, caring, in touch with the collective unconscious) in the presence of the client to produce change.

On the other hand many therapists totally disregard interpersonal skills. They give the impression that effective intervention in families requires merely the appropriate conceptual framework and a large set of technical skills. In our own early family therapy programs we essentially shared this somewhat naive view. However, several years of at times painful clinical feedback, coupled with productive and exciting research programs (Alexander & Barton, 1976; Alexander, Barton, Schiavo, & Parsons, 1976), have made it clear that specific therapist interpersonal skills are necessary to help families change, although they have little impact without a carefully structured conceptual framework and a well-developed set of technical skills.

In subsequent chapters we discuss each of these skill categories in detail and offer guidelines for deciding on their form and predicting their impact. Our basic position is that family theory and therapy provide the most useful conceptual framework for a therapist, even though they may not be directly utilized. When individuals or subsystems such as a mother and child are seen, the therapist should still consider and integrate the father and siblings in developing treatment strategies (Weakland et al., 1974). To use but one simple example, a program designed to reduce a son's aggression toward his mother may fail to produce change if the father wants to have an aggressive son. Individualized behavior programs—assertiveness training, relaxation training, and other treatment programs performed out of the context of the natural or relevant social system—must take into account the impact new behaviors will have on the social system, particularly the family. If the family is unable or unwilling to favorably respond to new behaviors, chances are that gains made by an individual will not be reinforced and maintained in the natural environment. In fact, they may be actively opposed. Thus, programs that ignore the larger environment produce mixed results at best.

In sum, as Madanes and Haley (1977) argued, family therapy is more of an orientation than a specific method. In this book, however, we take a somewhat more restricted focus in describing how to think about, change, and relate directly to a variety of family types and forms. We describe specific methods and specific therapist styles. Our goal is to help family therapists develop both the certainty and the flexibility required to meet the complex and powerful demands of families in distress.

CHAPTER 1

Understanding the Principles of Family Functioning

This chapter is not designed to describe everything that a family is but to introduce a particular way of looking at families. Our aim is to provide a perspective that will help therapists unravel the complexity of families so that they can quickly and effectively develop means for helping families solve their problems.

Why are concepts so important? Why not begin this book with a discussion of change techniques (the tools of the trade) or of service delivery (the therapist as change agent)? After all, concepts don't change families, therapists using certain techniques do. However, change will be at best chaotic and often a result of luck if therapists enter the family arena with a complex set of techniques and styles but without a conceptual framework to guide them. Without this framework, therapists are hard pressed to address the right issues at the right time. When should they focus on problem behavior rather than emphasizing relationships? When should they gently guide a family to understanding? How do they recognize a destructive interaction, and when should they forcefully interrupt such an interaction? Therapists must make many such crucial decisions. When they make them correctly, family change can be surprisingly easy; but, when they make the wrong decisions, families experience only variable progress at best.

CONTEXTUAL PERSPECTIVE

How can a therapist decide what is important? Unfortunately, each family has its own set of rules for functioning and therefore different ways of changing. A family is a group of individuals with unique histories, feelings, and needs and with specific ways of behaving in specific settings. But each member can be understood only in relation to each other member. Change can result from understanding and changing any one member, but efficient and reliable change results only when therapists understand how all members interact with one another. To gain this understanding, therapists must view not only each individual and his or her behavior but the relationships among individuals as well (Haley, 1969; Watzlawick, Beavin, & Jackson, 1967; Watzlawick, Weakland, & Fisch, 1974). For example, a marriage partner can be effectively dominant only with a submissive spouse. And, as many parents have found, being in control of adolescents depends a great deal on how much adolescents allow themselves to be controlled; the apparently dominant act of giving orders is anything but dominant if the orders are ignored or (even worse) countermanded. Problems arise not because of what people are (dominant, hostile, withdrawn) but because others do not accept the way they interact. In one family a child may be labeled hyperactive because parents cannot tolerate the behavior, while in another family parents may proudly interpret the very same behavior as a sign of independence and assertiveness. Or, as we know from popular syndicated newspaper columns, some wives complain because their husbands are highly sexual, while others complain because their husbands are not. Behavior, then, takes meaning only from the context in which it occurs.

Viewing behavior in its context is perhaps the single most important skill the family therapist must have, but it is easy to lose this perspective in the intensity of family therapy sessions. In our own clinic, for example, a 6'4" father recently glared at a 24-year-old, 5'2" female therapist and threatened "You can't tell me what to do, you don't even have kids." Even though she was skilled in maintaining a contextual perspective, it was hard for her to avoid feeling attacked and thinking in individualistic and blaming terms, such as "He *is* a chauvinist, he *is* defensive, he *is* an SOB." Yet, to be effective, the therapist had to retain her contextual perspective and attribute father's behavior not to some individual trait or state but to his relationships with others at the time. In this case, she replied: "Oops, you just told me to lay off just the way Mom told you to lay off a few minutes ago when she almost screamed that you could never understand her feelings as a mother. It sounds like everyone kind of feels they've got 'special territory' that others just can't understand. Do you two *want* to understand each other?" By responding this way, the therapist turned the focus back to the marital relationship and did not keep the focus on herself by defending her position as a therapist. Other responses might have worked as well or perhaps even better; therapists must use responses that fit their own styles. However, to consistently be effective, therapists must make relationships the critical focus and continually think in relational and contextual terms.

To help ourselves and our trainees understand families and their members in relational terms, we often use an analogy to music. In fact, therapists often use the same word found in music —harmonious—to describe families that blend together well and require no help to do so as opposed to discordant families that probably need help. Of course, just as musical harmony is a subjectively defined phenomenon, so professionals often disagree as to which families are harmonious. Nevertheless, this relational phenomenon is real, and its absence is quite obvious.

How can families, like musicians, attain harmony? Isolated musical notes, like isolated behaviors, are meaningless by themselves; what most of us remember and hum to ourselves are certain sequences of notes called melodies or tunes. Some family therapists, like some music teachers, try to assure us that while isolated behaviors, or notes, are indeed nothing, sequences, or tunes, are everything: sequences that lead up to and follow tantrums (or drinking or refusal to have sex) are all we need to understand and modify. But this simply is not true. Therapists have come to realize that there is more to understanding families than understanding sequences of behavior. We use the term *theme* to describe those total relationships that define a family. Therapists must understand themes in order to change families, just as composers must understand and orchestrate themes in order to make music.

Unfortunately, themes in families are often difficult to define just as in music they may often be difficult to perceive. This difficulty may be due in part to a lack of appreciation or understanding. The acid rock of the 1970s seemed to have no rhyme or reason to people who preferred the big-band era, but it was understandable to many teenagers. Difficulty in defining themes may also be due to the wide variety of dimensions that must be taken into account. Many symphonies are played today exactly as they were more than a century ago, and the true connoisseur can notice a single note misplayed by the second French horn player. The particular form of the themes is predictable and reliable. In fact it can be argued that the form is the theme. In contrast, musical groups playing jazz and Dixieland seem to share some implicit understanding of the theme but shun orderliness and predictability for the sake of spontaneity. Despite few musical rules the performers all finish at the same time, the different parts all fit together, and to many of us it even sounds good. In this form of music the form of the piece varies greatly from playing to playing. Even though different groups play the same song, the differences are often greater than the similarities. Similar variability in the behavior of families is probably one of the reasons it has been so difficult to come up with useful family typologies.

This musical analogy reflects a major philosophical underpinning of this book. Family therapy—intervention in families designed to produce positive change—is a complex undertaking. Family therapy is an orchestration requiring talent, hard work, and normally a fair amount of training on the part of the person doing the orchestrating. It cannot be done by everyone, nor should it be. And being skilled in individual therapy, group therapy, or other approaches does not imply that one is skilled in family therapy any more than being a great ragtime pianist implies that one can play with a symphony orchestra.

While trainees find our analogy of family interaction to a musical composition compelling, the analogy breaks down at one crucial point. Musical notes don't come together by themselves, create new little notes, change and interact with various combinations of even more notes, and at some point in time throw themselves together to mutually create a coherent theme. Yet this is exactly what family members characteristically do—they create the themes themselves. Unlike a passive note, each person has an active impact, sometimes incompatible, on the theme. The point at which a therapist typically sees a family is when the themes are no longer harmonious but have instead become discordant. Characteristically in this situation someone decides that the themes are wrong, crazy, bad, or illegal. Unfortunately, while a song writer can simply rearrange passive notes and sequences to attain a more desirable theme, family therapists rarely find all members so willingly changed.

Where does this leave the aspiring family therapists? In a later section we describe a number of themes that can provide guidelines for family therapists, but we must first introduce an additional level of analysis, the concept of function, or the reasons family members relate to one another the way they do.

FUNCTIONS OF BEHAVIOR

Obviously, musical notes don't care what their relationships are. But people do care and work hard to create, maintain, or terminate relationships. As we will see later in this chapter, people develop characteristic cultural, physical, environmental, and interpersonal ways to regulate their relationships (Altman & Taylor, 1973; Beier, 1966). The concept of function helps the therapist see how each of the members of a particular family accomplishes this end.

Putting aside fancy concepts for a moment, we believe that family therapists, when viewing a set of problematic interactions, should ask one simple question: When the smoke cleared, what was the result of these interactions from a relational standpoint —what was their function in regulating relationships within this family? By asking this question, therapists can often can insight into what family members cannot or will not tell them. For example, squabbling with her teenage daughter characteristically results in a mother's hysteria, which finally pulls the father out of his workshop and into a disciplining role. Here, we assert that one function of the argument is to force the father into contact. In contrast, if the father characteristically storms off to the office because he "can't get any work done in this turmoil," then we assert that one function of the argument is to create distance for the father. To use another common example, if a worried mother constantly checks her daughter's pockets for dope or pills and the daughter reliably engages in extended arguments about the intrusion, we assert that one function of the interaction is to provide the mother with contact and a sense of having a mothering role. Clinicians notice that mothers who maintain contact with their daughters as they grow older (share information, shop together) aren't the ones who snoop. However, some mothers cannot accept the lessening of their mothering role when their daughters begin to grow away and no longer treat them as mothers. In response, these mothers try to reestablish their role through such tactics as snooping and setting curfews. For them, the resulting battles function to preserve their mothering roles, though in ways that are certainly less than optimal, efficient, or pleasant.

To understand the concept of function is a challenge for the new family therapist. It is difficult to see that a mother's crying and wringing her hands because of her daughter's truancy is a way of maintaining a relationship. Yet the following excerpted case summary clearly demonstrates how the mother's actions do function in this way.

> Mother reports that Debbie, 14 years old, has been receiving increasingly poor grades for 18 months. Within the past 12 months she has begun smoking dope; has been having sexual relations with her 19-year-old, unemployed boyfriend; has almost stopped going to school; and rarely comes home except late at night. At home she is sullen, argumentative, occasionally hysterical, and rarely truthful.

How can the mother be anything but a victim of this girl's pathology? A review of a characteristic sequence provides a clue.

> At 4:30 P.M. Debbie comes home, changes clothes without speaking, and begins to walk out of the house. Mother, obviously annoyed, says, "Where do you think you're going? You haven't cleaned your room for days, you've done no homework, and I doubt if you even went to school today."
>
> Debbie responds, with sarcasm, "I'm going to Suzie's." Mother and Debbie then begin arguing about the "truth" of each other's subsequent accusations, the appropriateness of each other's motivations, and the like. Finally Mother makes an indirect accusation about Debbie's sexual activity with her boyfriend, to which Debbie responds: "At least I'm not so old that I forgot how." Mother responds by slapping Debbie, who wrenches away and runs indignantly out the door.

This sequence, though rich in specific behavior events, is for the family therapist an incomplete picture, for it fails to describe the larger familial context in which it occurs. Although we can guess that the function of Debbie's behavior is to create a justification for running away, the sequence as yet provides little information about a possible interpersonal payoff for the mother. Thus the therapist must find out how this typical sequence affects all relationships in the family.

> At 6:45 P.M. Father comes home (somewhat late, as had been increasingly occurring).

Mother, in a highly agitated voice: "You've got to do something about Debbie."

Father, exasperated: "Like what?"

Mother: "I don't know—something."

Father, sarcastically: "I suppose I should quit my job so *I* can be home to take care of the kids."

Mother, angry and whining: "Forget it. If you don't care if she ends up pregnant, then just don't do nothin'."

This comment pushes Father's button, and he spends the remainder of the evening fuming. When Debbie finally returns home at 11:30 P. M., Father begins yelling at her; when she responds sarcastically, he slaps her several times until she runs into her room sobbing.

Mother and Father then mutually discuss Debbie's many "shortcomings," with Mother comforted by Father's intervention and Father relieved that Mother is no longer complaining about his lack of involvement.

By looking at Debbie's behavior in the context of other (marital) relationships, we can see a coherent picture beginning to emerge. Debbie's behavior, although certainly a problem, begins to look also like a tool used by Mother to force Father into action, despite Mother's description of the problem in which she blames Debbie totally. Father rarely had the responsibility for parenting while Debbie was younger, and he has no idea about what can be done at this stage of family development. Thus he characteristically withdraws until Mother threatens that his inaction will result in dire consequences, and this threat coerces him into (admittedly ineffective) action. Thus we can hypothesize that despite the misery of their situation, Mother may be receiving several payoffs: removal from responsibility because Father is forced to be the final authority; responsiveness from Father, which Mother doesn't receive if she handles the situation by herself; and maintenance of her mothering role.

Thus to understand families therapists must look beyond the apparent problem and refocus on all relationships. In this process, they must often go beyond the motives people verbalize and focus instead on the interpersonal results—the function of the behavior. Only by understanding both the context and functions of problematic behavior can therapists develop plausible hypotheses about why family members contribute to interactions that on the surface seem to create misery for all of them (Stanton, 1980a). In Debbie's family, Mother feared the loss of contact and support that was resulting from the children's growing away. This fear prompted behavior that replaced the loss with support from Father. And, although this support involved turmoil, without it she would have been totally isolated from her departing children and a characteristically distant husband. Admittedly many mothers handle this transition by creating different alternatives (such as affairs, new careers, club work, or adaptive renegotiation of the marital relationship), but this woman's learning history and expectations (cultural and religious, to name but two) did not allow her to do so without external assistance.

This oversimplified vignette will be fleshed out later with detailed explanations. At this point we do not expect the reader to possess a well-integrated understanding of the model we are proposing. This introductory section is designed to show how we view family members and their behaviors as a highly interdependent set of relationships. We first view individuals and the patterns of their interactions to see what they do to or with each other. In musical terms, we need to know the notes and the tune. Then we view the patterning of these sequences to understand family themes. From these themes, we then try to ascertain the function of maladaptive sequences for each family member in order to understand why each continues to participate in what most agree are unpleasant events. Sadly, in some families the father has an impact only when he comes home drunk; the son gets freedom only by running away; or the teenage daughter shows love for her mother only after the mother has lost an argument with the father. An understanding of these functions is necessary for the therapist to design specific change programs for specific behaviors and specific sequences.

TYPES OF INTERPERSONAL FUNCTIONS

At one level, the interpersonal payoffs or functions that family members attain appear to be many: a chauvinistic husband prevents his wife from developing an independent career by ensuring that the turmoil at home keeps her there; a child elicits parental attention by having a tantrum; a teenager creates independence by having himself thrown out of the house; a spouse avoids arguments by being excessively busy at work. Yet, although these themes have a wide variety of forms, in the end they can be reduced to variations on two interpersonal states: contact/closeness (merging) and distance/independence (separating). Clinicians have discussed these states in other terms, such as "come here" versus "go away" and intimacy versus irresponsibility. Though these relational states are often seen as opposite ends on a single bipolar dimension, we have found it more useful to consider each as a separate dimension that ranges from low to high.

Therapists must be careful to avoid the same trap that family members produce for themselves by labeling either of these types of functions as good or bad. Because psychotherapy has evolved from models of ideal mental health, many therapists have developed concepts of functions that they implicitly or explicitly value as inherently good or bad. Closeness (or intimacy or openness) is generally seen as good, while independence (or distance or being closed) is seen as bad. But this need not be the case. "Smothering" may produce merging but in the nonadaptive form of enmeshment, which can lead to schizophrenic behavior and poor self-identity. Maintaining distance from other people may facilitate the development of independent thinking and a sense of autonomy and competence, which may be adaptive and effective styles of interaction both within the family and in the larger environment. Thus both types of functions are legitimate, although the specific ways people attain them may be unacceptable and thus have to be changed. The child who coerces attention (contact/closeness) by whining is not seen as bad because of the function that is created; the therapist's job is to modify the family system so that an alternative behavior (such as seeking advice in a friendly manner) can function to create contact/closeness. Family therapy is based on the notion that to produce this change other family members must also behave differently. This change is often easier suggested than accomplished because the other family members may be creating functions in ways that are incompatible with the child's new adaptive behavior. Thus the functional payoffs of all family members must be taken into account, legitimized, and translated into alternative specific behaviors that will produce an adaptive fit for them all.

Merging: Contact/Closeness

Behaviors and interpersonal styles that produce contact/closeness in a relationship tend to increase psychological intensity, enhance the opportunities for interaction, and maintain or strengthen contacts that would otherwise decrease. Typically (but not always) nonproblematic behaviors that function to increase contact/closeness include asking for or giving friendly help, crying, remaining close physically, and verbally and physically expressing tenderness ("I love you"). Family members can also create contact/closeness by manipulating aspects of the environment—leaving doors open rather than closed, dressing in an appealing manner, keeping room temperatures and noise at levels acceptable to other people.

It is impossible to create lists of behaviors that inevitably function to produce contact/closeness because, as the old saying goes, "One person's pain is another person's pleasure." The very same behavior that in one relationship produces merging can have the opposite effect in another relationship. Tender, sexual words and phrases may turn on spouse A but offend, frighten, or disgust spouse B. Thus while we can safely indicate that affection is a merging form of behavior for most families, we cannot know that holds true in any particular family until we see how the family operates. Theories can tell us what to look for and what we can probably expect, but they cannot tell us what is. Therapists must be particularly careful not to project their own interpretations of functions on family members. Many behaviors that function to produce contact/closeness for therapists may function in an opposite manner for the family members being seen.

Separating: Distance/Independence

This second major category of interpersonal functions includes behaviors that tend to decrease psychological intensity and dependence as well as physical and emotional contact. Colloquially speaking, these behaviors or styles send the message "You'd better do your thing on your own because I'm doing mine on my own."

As with merging, separating takes many forms. Some are acceptable to others, some unacceptable. The man who works two full-time jobs is absent from his family for long periods, but the added income may be sufficient reason for the others to find this degree of distance tolerable or even desirable. Another man may be gone for the same amount of time but spend it out drinking. Thus, although both men are separated from their families for equivalent periods of time, they tend to be evaluated differently. Other typical themes that produce distance/independence are intense arguing (although in some relationships arguing is an antecedent to making up and becoming closer), running away, being rigid, or compulsive or unresponsive, and keeping continually busy.

Midpointing

In many families, some or all members seem to characteristically behave in ways that consistently produce neither merging nor separating. Instead, elements of both functions seem to be concurrently present. The classic example of such behavior is the double bind of "come here" versus "go away." A less apparently pathological example is couples who do a lot together (merging) but only in groups (club activities, double dating). They maintain the component of distance/independence because the presence of other people tends to blunt the expression of high levels of intimacy and contact. The context creates a balance of contact and distance, which allows these couples to avoid the fear of being overwhelmed by intimacy yet at the same time not be isolated by distance. Other examples include the classic hysterical and depressed ("help me—yes, but") style that seems to midpoint interpersonal relationships with the simultaneous "come here"/ "go away" mixture. The affect expressed in this style tends to elicit nurturance (merging) from others, but when the nurturance doesn't help the situation others often begin to withdraw in frustration.

RELATIONSHIPS AMONG FUNCTIONS

Three aspects of human relationships complicate the understanding and assessment of interpersonal functions. First, as already mentioned, any given behavior is not inherently functional in a certain way. While expressing feelings may increase closeness in most relationships, for some people it is a frightening or otherwise aversive behavior that drives them away. The meaning of any behavior can thus be ascertained only in context.

Second, as seen in Figure 1-1, the functions are not clearly discrete; instead one blends into the other. In addition, the intensity of each varies from zero to large amounts. A child, for example, can maintain low levels of contact/closeness by occasionally talking quietly to a parent. The child can generate high levels of contact by active conversation or (on the coercive side) by whining and demanding attention. The child can generate very high levels through tantrums, picking on siblings, or being particularly appealing to a responsive parent. To identify the functional relationship between two people, then, the clinician must in a

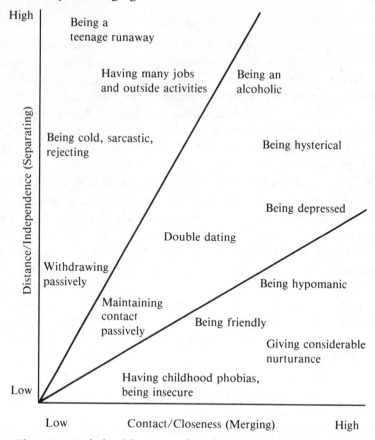

Figure 1-1. Relationships among functions illustrated by some typical behaviors.

sense do a frequency count of, or plot, functional reactions over time and identify the predominant direction of these reactions.

The third complicating factor is the fact that relationships exist in the context of other relationships. Any behavior that creates contact/closeness between A and B may at the same time create distance/independence between A and C. In fact, family members often behave in a certain way with one person in order to create a relational outcome with another person. For example, a father may soothe his sobbing daughter (merging) as a means of labeling the mother as a bitch (separating). As a result, therapists cannot simply list the traits of a person to identify functions. Functions exist only in the context of relationships, and the very same behaviors may be functionally different depending on the particular relationship in question. A father's careful attention and display of affection can elicit contact/closeness in one child (a child we might describe as dependent) yet create considerable distance in another (a teenager attempting to establish autonomy, for example).

FUNCTIONS AND COMMUNICATION

The global nature of the merging and separating framework has both advantages and disadvantages for family therapists. The advantage is that with experience therapists can take the complex interactions and unique behaviors of any family and describe them in similar, general terms. Because the terms are not behavior-specific, therapists can identify alternative behaviors that family members can perform that will have productive and pleasant results while continuing to maintain the functional payoff. For example, a father's separating from his wife now takes the form of starting arguments (which she doesn't like), but this behavior can be replaced with getting a second job (which may be accept-able to her).

The generality, however, of these functional terms can be problematic because the framework does not help the therapist understand how and why this particular behavior is developed by this particular person in this particular family. Why does one teenager create independence by running away, while another creates the independence by securing a job? To understand the specifics therapists must go beyond global identification of func-tions and identify the particular interactive behaviors, or moment-to-moment communications, that occur in families.

A major problem facing family therapists is the jump that must be made between what we see and what we must infer. Although such phenomena as observable behaviors, the arrange-ment of furniture, and the failure to act as expected (or desired) by others are overt, their meaning is our main concern. We can see someone crying, but we must infer whether he is crying be-cause he feels bad or because he is trying to intentionally manipu-late us or others through the use of tears. When we see someone comforting the cryer, we must again infer whether this behavior is part of a nurturing relationship or of a coercive relationship in which the comforter is forced to respond.

Society has developed rules or guidelines for efficiently and effectively demonstrating and inferring the meaning of behavior—we look sad when we experience a loss, and we cry when we experience pain. Even these patterns, though, are not universal.

Traditionally, for example, males have often not been allowed to cry in response to hurt, whereas females have often been given freedom to do so. In addition, therapists rarely see families when they are efficient and effective. Families in trouble have experienced a breakdown in the rules or guidelines for efficient and effective communication. Because of this breakdown, family therapists cannot make the usual inferences about relationships.

Communication is any process used by people to interact with their environment. It includes words, grimaces, arrangement of furniture, use of scents such as perfume, choice of clothing, and even the absence of an expected response such as not coming home when expected. These varied ways of communicating in themselves create difficulty in making inferences, and this difficulty is compounded with families in trouble, who not only do not use these ways of communicating effectively and efficiently but also often purposely distort messages. Couples say they want help but are looking for excuses to get a divorce. Delinquents promise to come home on time but already have plans to stay out late. To sort out meaning in the face of this complexity and distortion, the family therapist must understand the basic principles of human communication.

Principles of Communication

Because humans are social beings, our behavior is defined and heavily influenced if not determined by its interpersonal contexts. This basic assumption has two implications. First, it implies that behavior is not intrinsic in the sense that it is predetermined, unchangeable, and inflexible. People can change and do change as their interpersonal environment requires them to do so or when they wish to change that environment. Even the so-called rigid neurotic demonstrates wide variations in behavior as a result of variation in the environment. A second implication is that people cannot help but communicate. Everything we do and fail to do sends a message to those around us (Haley, 1963; Watzlawick, Beavin, & Jackson, 1967). Communication takes place in several channels simultaneously. First, the vocal channel consists of the unique vocal and linguistic patterns of an individual; it includes speaking loudly, softly, slowly, quickly as well as the words chosen and the general meaning of what is said. The second channel of communication is nonverbal behavior such as facial expressions and body posture. Third, we use the physical environment to communicate (Altman & Taylor, 1973). We close doors to create privacy; we place chairs together to create closeness. Fourth, we use such props as clothing to communicate—to look sexy or businesslike or motherly.

Because we can communicate in these various channels, we create yet another level of analysis—the fit among channels of communication. When a person says "I like you" (verbal) and has a warm smile (nonverbal), there is congruence between levels, and the person is in a position to take responsibility for the consequences of the behavior. When a person says "I love you" (verbal) but looks away disinterestedly (nonverbal), there is incongruence between levels, and responsibility is qualified or denied. This process of affirming or qualifying messages is called metacommunication (Haley, 1963; Watzlawick, Beavin, & Jackson, 1967). Metacommunication is a message about the literal content of a verbal message and may be verbal or nonverbal. It conveys the sender's attitude toward the messages just sent, himself or herself, and the receiver. For example, a person says "It has started to rain." In addition to giving this literal message, the person automatically comments at the metacommunicative level, by tone of voice (irritable or excited) or by facial or other body expressions (smile or frown) or by verbal explanation ("I wish the sun were shining"). Because nonverbal metacommunication is usually less clear than verbal communication and so requires greater attention for understanding, we typically believe the metacommunication and disregard the overt message. When our intimate partner says "I love you" in a disinterested voice and looks away, we invariably believe that our partner does not feel love. Incongruent communicating is a central component of problematic interactions.

Using Communication to Determine the Nature of a Relationship

Because communication depends on the interplay of two or more people, it allows us to infer two distinct phenomena: the nature of the relationship between them and the function of the communication for each of them. A basic rule of communication theory is that it is impossible for a person to avoid defining or taking control of the definition of his or her relationship with another (Haley, 1963). According to this rule not only are all messages reports but they also influence or command others. A statement such as "I feel bad today" is not merely a description of the internal state of the speaker; it expresses something like "Do something about this" or "Think of me as a person who feels bad." Every message from one person to another defines their relationship. Even if one tries not to influence another person by remaining silent, the silence becomes a factor in the interchange.

Communicative behavior defines a relationship as symmetrical or complementary (Haley, 1963). In a symmetrical relationship two people exchange the same type of behavior and do so on a roughly equal basis. Both people initiate action, criticize the other, offer advice. In a complementary relationship the two people—one in a superior position and the other in a secondary position—exchange different types of behaviors that complement each other. One gives and the other receives; one teaches and the other learns; one offers criticism and the other accepts it; one offers advice and the other follows it.

This division of relationships can be used to classify different relationships or different sequences within a particular relationship. Relationships may shift in nature rapidly (as when people take turns teaching each other), or they may shift slowly over time. A growing child progressively shifts from a complementary relationship with the parents, in which the transactions are almost exclusively parent-to-child, to a symmetrical relationship, in which transactions become adult-to-adult (Coles, Alexander, & Schiavo, 1974; Haley, 1963; Morton, Alexander, & Altman, 1976). This shifting from complementary to symmetrical relationships is a major focus of family therapy. It is part of the therapist's task to assess how each person is defining the nature of the relationship and why the respective definitions create conflict or other forms of inefficiency and pain.

The previously discussed example of Debbie's family illustrates this point. By making her own decisions, Debbie was providing a relationship definition ("I am no longer subordinate in a complementary relationship; I am redefining our relationship as symmetrical by determining my own plans for me just as you determine your own plans for you"). In this family, problems arose because Debbie's relationship definition was not congruent with Mother's. When Mother communicated messages such as "You'll go where I let you go," she was attempting to define the relationship as complementary ("I'm still superior"). In such circumstances symptoms often become the avenue for resolution. The therapist's task is to provide a different avenue.

In other situations the family members may not have incompatible relationship definitions, but they may be dissatisfied with the way in which the relationship definitions are being expressed. Both partners in a marriage may desire a complementary relationship—her superior, him subordinate—but he may resent her way of expressing superiority via condescending and belittling commands. In this instance the therapist has a somewhat easier task because the couple needs help only in modifying the style of communication rather than in resolving incompatible relationship definitions.

The Therapist's Role

Chapter 3 focuses on resolving incompatible definitions of the relationship, and Chapter 4 contains extensive descriptions of techniques for changing communication style. At this point we wish merely to point out that the family therapist must be an expert in the entire communication process for several reasons: to be a model of functional communication, to identify faulty communication patterns in clients, and to teach aspects of the communication process. The therapist must be able to teach the rules for clear communication, emphasize the necessity for family members to check out meanings given and received, and demonstrate how to recognize invalid assumptions being used as fact. In addition, knowledge of communication patterns can tell the therapist much about the nature of the relationships in a family and the reasons for unwanted behaviors. Thus, besides being a resource person with expertise in communication methods, the family therapist also acts as an official observer and a reporter in order to communicate what the family cannot see.

UNDERSTANDING RESISTANCE

As a therapist develops an interpersonal orientation while attending to the family structure, the possibility of predicting areas of conflict and stress within a family system is greatly increased. Of particular importance is the therapist's ability to predict, and even use, the resistance family members often produce when confronted with change. Many theoretical formulations have been offered to account for this resistance, which though predictable is often surprising in light of the apparent misery being experienced by the family. The concepts of relationship definitions and interpersonal functions can be used to explain this resistance. In a nutshell, family members can be seen as using the best means they have available to define their relationships in order to meet their functional needs. Though they may be aware of this process, quite often they are not; their behaviors and strategies are predictable and rule governed, but they are unaware of what the interaction rules are and why they behave as they do (Carson, 1969).

To return again to Debbie's family, Debbie's way of expressing her independence prevented Mother from maintaining control through her prior dominant role with her subordinate daughter. In response, Mother settled for a less pleasant situation but the only one in which she could still meet her needs to feel like a mother. This situation can turn into one of resistance if the therapist begins to help Debbie develop acceptable methods of growing up without at the same time allowing Mother to meet her mothering needs. In more colloquial terms, this particular woman would settle for being the mother of a delinquent girl rather than being no mother at all. Resistance, then, arises if the therapist begins to change one family member without simultaneously making certain the changes will allow others to maintain the functions they previously had.

A FAMILY SCHEMATIC

In the early stages of intervention, the therapist's picture of how family members' functions interrelate is necessarily tentative. However, without such a picture a therapist cannot begin to develop plans for change because change techniques will not be successful unless they are consistent with the functions of each family member. To provide a feel for how such relational pictures are developed, we present the schematic in Figure 1-2. It is the picture of functions that was developed by Debbie's family therapist after the second session.

Mother and Debbie

Debbie's characteristic behavior consistently increased her distance from Mother. She avoided coming home, used arguments as an occasion for leaving, and referred to behaviors such as sex that reliably distanced Mother. Mother's function was less clear. Her nagging, worrying, and attempting to set limits increased merging (without them she and Debbie had no interaction) but also increased separating because Mother's behaviors reliably resulted in Debbie's leaving. Thus both functions seemed to be present, leading the therapist to hypothesize a midpointing function, which despite Debbie's separating behavior still allowed

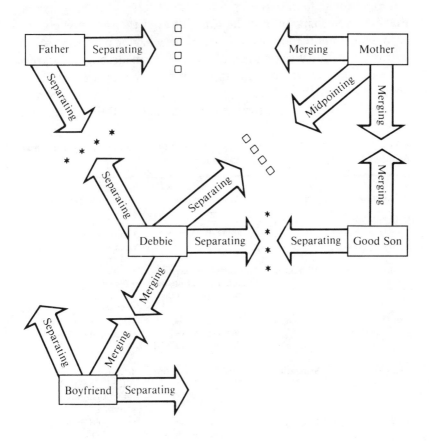

□
□ Incompatible functions
□

*
    Compatible functions but unacceptable behavioral manifestations
*

Figure 1-2. A functional schematic of Debbie's family.

Mother to maintain the mothering role that was so culturally important for her. An apparently irreconcilable mismatch between Mother's and Debbie's functions existed because midpointing and separating appear to be incompatible. Yet a therapist's attempts to change the functions of either mother or daughter would fly in the face of biology, their respective subcultures, and their deeply held attitudes.

Functional family therapy therefore uses a different strategy that involves changing not the functions but the specific behaviors used to maintain these functions. New behavior patterns are substituted for old (Weakland et al., 1974). If made creatively, these changes can avoid the incompatibility experienced by family members in distress and legitimize the functions of everyone involved. (See Table 1-1 for the changes made in Debbie's family.)

TABLE 1-1. Selected functions in Debbie's family and their behavioral manifestations before and during successful intervention.

Relationship	Interpersonal function	Behavioral manifestations	
		Preintervention	During intervention
Debbie-Mother	Separating	Is truant, is never home, runs away.	Is not truant, has Mother's permission to be away from home, brings reports and calls
Mother-Debbie	Midpointing	Contact via arguing and monitoring, distance via slapping and nagging.	Contact via reports and calls, distance via approved absence from home for specified times.
Mother-Father	Merging	Complains about Debbie, coerces Father into responding to her.	Holds daily discussion about family chart.
Father-Mother	Separating	Avoids home, refuses to respond.	Is allowed to fill Father role via family chart rather than direct interaction.
Mother-Good Son	Merging	Elicits and praises information about others' transgressions.	Elicits and praises information about others' accomplishments.
Good Son-Mother	Merging	Snoops and reports to Mother.	Reports positive accomplishments of others to Mother.
Debbie-Boyfriend Boyfriend-Debbie	Merging	Avoid school together and have evening contact.	Go to and from school together and have evening contact.
Debbie-Father Father-Debbie	Separating	Have almost no contact except for occasional intense arguing and hitting.	Have almost no contact; information is channeled through Mother.

Early in the intervention process, school performance was used successfully to maintain the functions of Mother and Debbie while changing the specific problematic behaviors. In return for her attending school, Debbie received unhassled approval for spending considerable time with her boyfriend (maintaining the merging function for both of them). Her initial willingness to do this was contingent in large part on her parents' promise not to have him charged with contributing to the delinquency of a minor. Once the family began experiencing rapidly improving relationships, however, this coercive component of the program was no longer necessary.

Debbie's going to school was only a small part of the change program because Mother's midpointing function had to be formally programed. In addition, the court required that Debbie's behavior be monitored, a requirement that had to be carefully designed in order to be effective yet still allow her to maintain her separating function. Thus an additional component of the program was brief class reports written by teachers. Debbie turned in these reports to Mother each day at 3:30 (maintaining a balance of separating and merging for Mother). As soon as Debbie turned in the reports, she was free to leave with her boyfriend (legitimizing her distancing from the family). In return for receiving parental approval for his involvement with Debbie, the boyfriend took Debbie to and from school, thus facilitating her attendance, and either brought her home for dinner or called Mother to inform her that Debbie wouldn't be coming. This part of the program was again designed to enhance Mother's merging but in an indirect form (midpointing). It also legitimized her need to know where Debbie was and was for her a much improved situation. (The boyfriend attended and participated in the early family sessions involving these arrangements so that his functions were also legitimized and incorporated.)

Father and Debbie and Mother

In their characteristic interactions, both father and daughter created distance, Debbie once again by being away whenever possible and Father by working late and being withdrawn and unresponsive at home. When finally forced into action by Mother, Father did such things as hit Debbie and take her to juvenile court.

Once again, some therapies might try to change both Debbie and her father in the hope they would become close and begin to have an ideal relationship. Although this is a noble goal, families already identified as hard core (Debbie had five referrals to juvenile court in a three-month period) drop out of therapy so frequently and have such high resistance and low motivation that basic changes are unrealistic. Functional family therapy thus creates alternative adaptive and acceptable ways for father and daughter to maintain their mutually agreed-on separating functions.

To allow Father and Debbie to maintain their separating functions and also to deal with the apparently incompatible father-separating, mother-merging functions, the device of a family chart was used. Mother's access to Father was legitimized and formalized by having her note daily on a chart Debbie's activities as well as those of the other children (only the "good" son, Tommy, is considered in Figure 1-2 and Table 1-1). She left the chart on the table for Father's perusal when he was up to it every day. This allowed Father to monitor family activity without having to directly face the intensity of a hysterical wife and out-of-control children (maintaining his separating function). He could even respond via written notes, but because his separating was legitimized and protected, with communication training he was able to increase direct communication and problem solving with his wife (maintaining her merging function).

Good Son

Prior to intervention, Tommy was relatively neutral with respect to Father and mildly antagonistic toward Debbie. His major investment was in the relationship with Mother. He was her baby, and they exchanged considerable affect and information. When discussing her children Mother made such remarks as "Thank God for Tommy." Tommy had become the family snoop, reporting both factual and rumored transgressions by the other children to Mother. He was lavishly praised for such activities by Mother but was disliked by the others, especially Debbie. The intervention program was designed to interrupt Tommy's part in destructive interaction but at the same time protect the Tommy/Mother contact/closeness function. This change was easily accomplished by helping Mother rearrange the content of Tommy's reports. Instead of reporting transgressions, Tommy was given the task of helping Mother monitor all the (carefully described) positive behaviors of the other children. Washed dishes, a mowed lawn, made-up beds, and completed school assignments were noted by Tommy and reported to Mother. The other children, who are not pictured in the schematic to avoid complexity, were rewarded for such activities by means that were functionally relevant for them. This program not only maintained the good son/mother merging relationship, but it improved Tommy's relationship with the other children and also helped Tommy learn that relationships need not always be maintained at the expense of someone else.

Outcomes

Once established, these programs created a positive momentum. As Mother nagged Debbie less and coerced Father less, Debbie spent more time at home and Father was more attentive. Conversely, as Debbie and Father became more responsive, Mother became more relaxed and pleasant. Also, as the boyfriend participated in Debbie's improved school performance, both parents saw him in an increasingly less negative light, and such activities as family picnics that included the boyfriend began occurring.

Finally, in what turned out to be the next-to-last session, Mother said she was concerned because her husband had become quite unaggressive sexually. The therapist scheduled the next session for the couple alone and promised them a program for improving sexual relationships. However, the couple arrived at the next session with smiles, occasional giggles (in stark contrast to the first session), and an enthusiastic insistence that the family no longer had problems they couldn't handle themselves.

Resistance, failed contracts, and unhappy affect have not been discussed in this case description nor have the therapeutic maneuvers that were necessary before the therapist could initiate the change programs. At this point in the book, these are the important points in this case history. First, the therapist began by hypothesizing the interpersonal functions. Second, these hypotheses presumed no one was evil, bad, or sick. Everyone's functions were legitimized, accepted, and separated from behavior. In this context, everyone could contribute to positive change. Third, the therapist designed change programs, based on these hypotheses, that left the functions intact but changed the ways in which they were maintained. Fourth, once the programs were instituted, the family began experiencing new positive interactions that gained in momentum and produced in turn additional beneficial changes. Finally, once a positive family momentum had been established, family members were able to reestablish adaptive and beneficial movements. Once their distance functions were legitimized and adaptive ways to maintain them were established, Debbie, her boyfriend, and Father all initiated merging behaviors. Debbie and her boyfriend seemed to need less distance from the family, and Father once again came home on time and participated in conversations with his wife. Mother stopped nagging and complaining, replacing that form of merging with problem solving and active listening. Debbie and her boyfriend still spent their time primarily alone; Father was still a relatively passive man;

and Mother was still the family worrier. After intervention, however, the family members were able to maintain adaptive and happy relationships in light of each other's needs and styles.

SUGGESTED READINGS

Ackerman, N. W. *The psychodynamics of family life.* New York: Basic Books, 1958. *Ackerman is often considered the grandfather of family therapy. For the systems purist this work is essential in order to understand the context out of which later family-systems therapies developed.*

Bertalanffy, L. von. *General systems theory: Foundation, development, applications.* New York: Braziller, 1948. *Though not focusing on families, the papers in this book provide the necessary conceptual underpinnings for later developments in family-systems theory. By bridging the physical and social sciences, von Bertalanffy demonstrates the wide applicability of systems-theory principles.*

Goldenberg, I., & Goldenberg, H. *Family therapy: An overview.* Monterey, Calif.: Brooks/Cole, 1980. *See comments on Okun and Rappaport (below).*

Gurman, A. S., & Kniskern, D. P. (Eds.). *Handbook of family therapy.* New York: Brunner/Mazel, 1980. *This handbook provides an excellent sample of the range of family intervention models and techniques. It raises and deals with critical issues in a scholarly yet clinically rich manner.*

Jackson, D. D. The study of the family. *Family Process,* 1965, 4, 1–20. *This article is one of the earliest statements of such basic principles as family rules and homeostasis. It may well be the single most influential article in the field.*

Jones, S. L. *Family therapy: A comparison of approaches.* Bowie, Md.: Brady, 1980. *This thoughtful and generally well-written comparative review provides the student with a broad overview of various family therapy perspectives. Unfortunately, the book is marred by instances of misleading interpretations of research findings. These instances include a complete omission of the major treatment condition in two classic family therapy outcome studies.*

Okun, B. F., & Rappaport, L. J. *Working with families: An introduction to family therapy.* North Scituate, Mass.: Duxbury, 1980. *This book and Goldenberg and Goldenberg (above) are excellent overviews. They provide the beginning family therapy student with a comprehensive description of various theoretical and applied aspects of family assessment and intervention. They provide a solid basis for subsequently gaining the detailed knowledge necessary to perform family therapy. The accompanying workbooks engage the students in a range of didactic and experiential exercises that promote knowledge of specific conceptual, technical, and relationship variables in family treatment.*

Watzlawick, P., Beavin, J. H., & Jackson, D. D. *Pragmatics of human communication.* New York: Norton, 1967. *The careful organization and clear presentation of basic principles of human communication in this book provide excellent background for later works. The book persuasively describes how deviant behavior is an interactive, not intrapsychic, phenomenon.*

CHAPTER 2

Deciding What
to Change:
Assessment

Before we discuss in detail the two major components of the functional family model—therapy and education—we need to recognize that both need to be performed in a meaningful context. The techniques used in these two phases show how families can be changed, but they do not indicate what should be changed. Thus, the first phase of intervention, assessment, is necessary to develop targets for change.

Assessment generally follows one of two major models: the pretherapy, historical approach or the here-and-now, ongoing approach. The pretherapy approach is based on the assumption that to produce change one must uncover the dynamic causes of family themes, which can then be used to guide intervention. In this approach, the therapist identifies (through interviews, tests, behavioral observations) individual capacities, needs, and the like and then fits them together in an attempt to understand the reasons for current symptoms.

Although this approach is thorough, it can be inefficient, and as pointed out by Haley (1976) it may even contribute to poor therapeutic outcomes. Family therapists have found the first one or two sessions to be critical; if a family fails to experience immediate change during these critical sessions, part or all of the family may refuse to continue in treatment. Therefore, even though the information gained through pretherapy assessment may be useful, a poorly motivated family often drops out before therapy is initiated or even before assessment is complete.

Pretherapy assessment also tends to create defensiveness and resistance that cannot be dealt with effectively. The problem person, or identified patient, tends to remain thoroughly ensconced in that role. Other family members, in turn, are almost forced to maintain their roles as victims because the therapist has not yet redefined their relationships and dealt with the unwanted consequences of their behavior.

As a result of these constraints, functional family therapists opt for the here-and-now assessment approach. We assess and intervene simultaneously, entering the family and assessing not only who they are—demographic features, history—but perhaps more important, how they react to our attempts at change (Haley, 1971; Stanton, 1980b)—how they respond to the various therapeutic and educational intervention described in the next two chapters. This approach has several ramifications. It is difficult for the casual observer to separate assessment from intervention, as these two processes are intertwined and simultaneous. Although this procedure may create confusion for the trainee, it comforts the family because they are being helped while they are being assessed. In addition, the therapist, even during assessment, can set the stage for intervention, establish the rules for therapy, and have an impact based on what the therapist does instead of on a promise of what will happen after assessment.

In sum, then, assessment is not a distinctly different initial phase but is part and parcel of the change process itself. However, for purposes of clarification, this chapter identifies several particular goals and techniques of assessment as if they were independent and occurred prior to introducing the techniques for initiating change described in the next chapter.

IDENTIFYING FUNCTIONS

The identification of functions has been discussed already and will receive additional attention in later chapters. However, because functions are such an important part of family intervention and because identifying functions is a complex and subtle art, we feel some repetition is appropriate.

Consider the teenager who gets into trouble only when out with peers. When at home or alone in school or at the market, she behaves in an appropriate and acceptable manner. Based on the behavioral literature, one could argue that this is a case of stimulus control and that the solution is to prevent the teenager from being in the presence of peers. No sensible family therapist, however, would attempt such a solution because with most teenagers it not only wouldn't work but would most likely create additional problems. According to the functional family model, contact with peers serves two powerful and understandable functions: separating from the family and merging with peers. Although the form of the specific behaviors is problematic, it is appropriate and necessary for the teenager to develop these two functions adaptively in her movement toward adulthood (Morton, Alexander, & Altman, 1976). As a result, any attempted solution that reduced separating from the family and merging with peers would face strenuous resistance. Instead, the family therapist must help the family develop alternative acceptable ways for this teenager to maintain both functions. This, of course, is no easy task and often requires considerable creativity on the part of therapists and family members alike.

This example is also a reminder that to identify functions a therapist must view extrafamilial relationships as well as those internal to the family. It is not uncommon, for example, for a spouse to create turmoil within the marriage as a way of maintaining contact/closeness with his or her own parents. "Going home to Mama" allows both the spouse and his or her parents to enjoy a powerful merging function that they cannot maintain through any other means. Many husbands who would otherwise be called "Mamas' boys" can legitimize going home only by leaving a troubled marriage. In a similar vein, a mother may be seen as meddling in a child's stable marriage, but, if the marriage is discordant, then her involvement can be legitimized ("What else can a mother do?").

The naive therapist who ignores such extrafamilial functions will experience considerable confusion and a lack of progress because people's behavior often becomes apparently irrational when relational payoffs are not considered in change programs. One marriage therapist stated: "I have taught this guy how to communicate and negotiate, and his wife is willing to do more of the things he wants in exchange for his attention and his coming home on time. Yet he continues to blow up at silly little things. Perhaps we should consider a mild tranquilizer." Any change attempt that fails to legitimize extrafamilial functions or fails to develop alternative acceptable ways for them to be maintained will elicit similar resistance.

Finally, family therapists must be constantly aware of the fact that they, too, are part of a set of functional relationships within the family. Traditional transference and countertransference are manifestations of these functional relationships and can be powerful traps for the therapist. A seductive husband may ensure that his wife fails by simultaneously maintaining distance from her and closeness with the female therapist. If the female therapist becomes flattered by this attention and tries to model appropriate merging behaviors for the wife, such as being pleasant and attentive, the therapist may be maintaining a powerful functional payoff for the husband's distance from his wife. In sum, as soon as interactional patterns have been identified, the therapist should begin to hypothesize the nature of the functional outcomes within the family, in extrafamilial relationships, and in the therapeutic context itself.

MAJOR TECHNIQUES FOR
ASSESSING FAMILY INTERACTIONS

The therapy and research literature abounds with theoretical and empirical disputes about the relative importance of feelings, behavior, and thoughts as a focus of intervention. For the functional family therapist, however, this dispute is irrelevant because our predominant focus is the fit among family members—the relational qualities of their interactions. Thus, behavior sequences, feelings, and cognitions are equally viable modes through which the therapist can assess the nature of intrafamily relationships. Family members simultaneously behave in sequences and have feelings and have thoughts. However, family members may emphasize different modes. Some report very concrete behaviors. ("Every Tuesday she cuts out of school after free period and goes with her girlfriend to the park. Then they usually find some boys and end up smoking dope.") Others present generalized attributions. ("He's lazy. He just doesn't care. His attitude is ruining the family.") Other members report behaviors, feelings, and cognitions. Therapists can use all these modes to develop the relational picture of the family and set the stage for intervention, as can be seen in Figure 2-1. (To simplify, we consider feelings and cognitions as one mode because they cannot be directly observed and must be inferred from behavior or verbal report.)

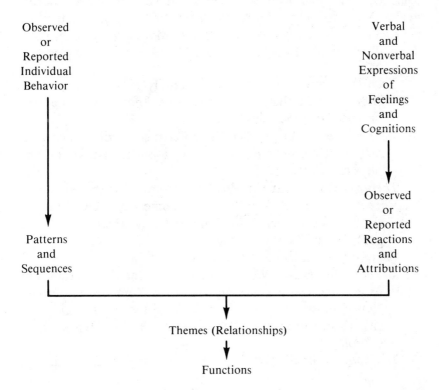

Figure 2-1. Assessment modes.

Behaviors, feelings, and cognitions can be looked at during the therapy session itself or as they occur outside of sessions. Instead of worrying endlessly about the extent to which in-therapy behavior mirrors the real nature of the family, functional family therapists focus on whichever context is more accessible and easier for the therapist to deal with. Ultimately, the family must learn to be an efficient problem-solving unit at home as well as in the therapist's office, but during assessment it matters little where the focus is. Let's look now at how assessment modes can be utilized by the therapist, focusing first on the process at home and then on the process during a therapy session.

Behavior Sequences as an Entry Mode

Consider Mother, Father, and Carol, their 12-year-old daughter, referred by the family pediatrician. Carol has been experiencing debilitating gastrointestinal upset and pain, yet several complete medical work-ups have revealed no organic cause. As the symptoms worsen and no physical cause can be determined, Mother becomes increasingly anxious and depressed and finally develops neurodermatitis. Father is an engineer, Mother a university student; all family members are physically attractive and articulate.

> *Therapist* (entering room with family): Please be seated. (Looks at Mother.) Does everyone know you called me because Dr. Jones suggested I might help?
>
> *Mother:* Yes . . . uh . . . Carol's problem is . . . ah . . . he thinks maybe it's psychological. There doesn't seem to be any physical reason for it.
>
> *Therapist* (looking at Father): What seems to be the problem?
>
> *Mother:* Her stomach aches. She's home from school two or three times a week now. I never know when the nurse is going to call.
>
> *Therapist:* What happens when she does?
>
> *Mother:* The nurse? Well . . . I . . . sometimes she wasn't able to get me 'cause I was at school, so Tom had to get her. Now I mostly stay home. I dropped two classes. Or else I give them my friend's number, and I call her when I'm at school.
>
> *Therapist:* Uh-huh. (Looks at Father, then at Carol, then at Father.)
>
> *Father:* I just couldn't keep being interrupted. This computer thing at work is a mess.
>
> *Therapist:* So you aren't able to help out very much.
>
> *Father:* No . . . I just. . . .
>
> *Therapist* (interrupts, looks at Mother): And you end up having to drop classes. Have you always been the one responsible for Carol?

At this point Carol begins to blink tears, and the atmosphere in the room becomes heavy yet not sullen. It becomes clear to the family that they are a network, with each of them having an impact on the others. The therapist has focused almost exclusively on behavior and sequences to identify one major relational theme: Mother is the parent responsible for Carol. There is much more to be learned, of course, including the function of this theme for each family member. Our main concern here is to demonstrate how a focus on behaviors and sequences can be used to identify a relational component in the family.

Feelings and Cognition as an Entry Mode

In contrast, the therapist might have focused on the emotional and cognitive aspects of family life to tease out the nature of relationships.

Therapist (entering room with family): Please be seated. (Looks at Mother.) Does everyone know you called me because Dr. Jones suggested I might help?

Mother: Yes . . . uh . . . Carol's problem is . . . ah . . . he thinks maybe it's psychological. There doesn't seem to be any physical reason for it.

Therapist (looking at Father): What seems to be the problem?

Mother: Her stomach aches. She's home from school two or three times a week now. I never know when the nurse is going to call.

Therapist: So the whole thing just keeps you up in the air.

Mother: Yes . . . I . . . ah . . . I can't make any plans to be away.

Therapist: So this has really had a big impact on you?

Mother: Oh, yes . . . I . . . .

Therapist (interrupts, looks at Father): What is your reaction to all this?

Father: It has upset all of us.

Therapist: In what way?

Father: Well . . . she really feels frustrated; she was upset about having to drop classes.

Therapist: At the university?

Father: Yes. Someone has to be home in case she has another attack.

Therapist: Let me see now. (Looks at Carol.) It seems that your stomach problems have really affected your mom. Has she always been the one you felt close to?

At this point Carol begins to blink tears, and, just as in the previous vignette, the family sees itself as an interdependent network—this time of feelings and responsibilities. In this instance the therapist has focused primarily on feelings and reactions, yet has created the same relational picture of the family. Once again the therapist has identified a major theme: Mother is the parent with the most immediate emotional ties to Carol.

Both these vignettes focused on reports about the family at home. The therapist, however, could have instead focused on in-session patterns.

> *Therapist* (entering room with family): Please be seated. (Looks at Mother.) Does everyone know you called me because Dr. Jones suggested I might help?
>
> *Mother:* Yes . . . uh . . . Carol's problem is . . . ah . . . he thinks maybe it's psychological. There doesn't seem to be any physical reason for it.
>
> *Therapist* (looking at Father): What seems to be the problem?
>
> *Mother:* Her stomach aches. She's home from school two or three times a week now. I never know when the nurse is going to call.
>
> *Therapist* (looking at Father): You know, it's interesting that, when I asked you what the problem was, your wife answered.
>
> *Mother and Father* (overlapping): No, she just/I thought that . . . .
>
> *Therapist* (looking at both): Oops, I didn't mean to make you feel like you had to defend yourselves. I just wondered why.
>
> *Mother:* Well, I . . . I'm the one who is closer to the situation.
>
> *Therapist:* How's that?
>
> *Mother:* Well, since it happens mostly during the day, I'm the one who has to be there for the nurse to call.
>
> *Therapist:* I see. Father, were you aware she had answered for you?
>
> *Father:* Uh . . . no, not really. She's more talkative than I am, so I guess I'm used to it.
>
> *Therapist:* Uh-huh . . . well, for whatever reason, it seems that Mom seems to be more in the middle of all this than Dad.

Focusing on Relationships

The important aspect of this style is that, while deemphasizing the content of what was said, the therapist in all three examples used the interaction to focus on the relationships among family members. The therapist avoided an individualistic focus; the therapist did not pursue why Dad is less talkative but only that as a result Mom seems to be more in the middle.

It is crucial also that the therapist restrict discussion to patterns of behavior or feelings and not open it up to the reasons one person behaves or feels as he or she does. Family members often spend a great deal of time accusing one another, and the therapist must avoid adding to this destructive momentum (see Chapter 3). Thus at this stage the therapist did not ask why Father's work is more important than Mother's school; instead the therapist pointed out that Mother is the person responsible for Carol. Similarly, the therapist didn't ask why Mother cuts Father off; instead the therapist pointed out the interdependent nature of the family members' behaviors, feelings, and thoughts.

FORMAL ASSESSMENT TOOLS

We have so far described the assessment approach as involving direct observation of interaction patterns in the therapy sessions and verbal descriptions of behavior and feelings in the natural environment. We have emphasized that the therapist must create a relational picture of the family that describes the interdependence of the members. Our major initial interest thus is not why family members relate in the way they do but how they relate. Nonetheless, once the how of family interrelatedness is identified, the therapist, in order to develop adaptive alternatives, must generate ideas as to why family members have adopted the particular patterns they have. To do so, the therapist may continue to utilize verbal descriptions of out-of-session behaviors and feelings by the family members, nonverbal cues such as sweating, and in-session interactions. The therapist may also use two general types of assessment devices—diagnostic testing and direct in vivo (home) observation—to fill in the blanks.

Diagnostic Testing

Diagnostic tests vary on a number of dimensions including format (objective or projective), goals (measurement of attitudinal configuration or interests or intelligence), scoring procedures (profile or subjective interpretation), and focus (individual characteristics or family outcomes). Because this is not a text on diagnostic assessment, we shall not address problematic issues such as reliability and validity, nor shall we inventory the many tests. Instead, we shall assume that therapists are aware of the range and potential limitations of these tests and discuss instead the context in which they can be used.

Diagnostic tests usually cannot describe interpersonal functions, but they can provide a partial answer as to why particular interactions are used in a family. They can tell us about the internal constraints on behavior, feelings, and attitudes of each member. For example, an intelligence test cannot indicate how a son's truancy is used by his mother to force his father to interact with the son (by reprimanding him or helping him with his schoolwork or whatever). However, an intelligence test can indicate whether the son is bright enough to understand the material he is encountering in school.

As a specific example, in the early stages of assessment a therapist identified one of several themes in a family with a truant son. Each time Jimmy fouled up (was truant or was given a failing grade), Mother became involved in meeting with counselors. Father was typically distant, busy building his professional practice. After each incident, however, Mother somewhat forcefully and frantically demanded that Father do something, adding suggestions she had gleaned from her meetings with counselors. Father in turn confronted Jimmy with a lecture on such topics as responsibility, dedication, and postponement of gratification.

The therapist realized that this typical sequence served numerous family functions, including giving Mother access to Father (through giving him suggestions and forcing him to interact with Jimmy). The therapist was also able to confirm the hypothesis that busy Father was not readily available to Mother or to Jimmy unless there was a crisis to be solved. The therapist could thus assume that the son's truancy served important family (especially marital) relationship functions. Why truancy, though? Why not sarcasm toward Mom or the blatant use of drugs? To answer this question, the therapist requested an intelligence test which showed that Jimmy was of only low-normal intelligence; thus he became easily intimidated by schoolwork and left school to avoid aversive outcomes. The information on Jimmy's intelligence also helped the therapist understand why Father's lectures had no constructive effect: Jimmy was not sufficiently bright to understand the abstractions that Father typically used.

Thus the intelligence test helped ascertain why the particular symptom of truancy was developed by the son. In a similar vein, a projective device that identifies a man's sexual fears can help a therapist understand why the man uses impotence to maintain distance from his wife. Information from the broad range of diagnostic tests can have similar fill-in-the-blank functions.

We must emphasize, however, that most family therapists, ourselves included, use diagnostic tests only infrequently. As mentioned above, they often reinforce the concept of the problem person—a concept that the family must change. Also, the information they provide can often be obtained more easily and directly through careful observation, questioning, and prompting. Finally, family therapists are leery of being trapped by the individualistic focus of most diagnostic tests, fearing that too heavy a reliance on such tests will blind them to the relational impact of behaviors.

Direct Home Observation

Numerous family therapists, particularly those classified as behavior modifiers, have developed standardized coding schemes to be used by trained observers in the home setting. These coding schemes have been particularly useful in identifying interdependent sequences of behaviors that occur at a high rate, as in the case of aggressive children (Patterson & Reid, 1970). Other therapists have developed individualized coding schemes to evaluate a range of problem situations including marital arguments, dysfunctional problem solving, bedtime conflicts, and the granting of privileges to adolescents. Independent judgments about the components of such typical problematic sequences can be helpful when family members are confused or disagree about how sequences erupt and evolve.

Once again, however, such information can blind the therapist to the dynamic relational components that maintain family problems. To return to an earlier example, a careful description of the truant son's sullenness during Father's lecturing can provide a precise analysis of the interdependence of the lecturing and sullenness with one leading to the other until Father leaves in frustration. But, without a functional view, the therapist may miss the fact that Father's behavior is the result of Mother's prodding, not simply his reaction to Jimmy's sullenness.

A similar problem occurs when family members are causal but absent. A mother may abuse her child only when she feels helpless and frustrated because the father (who is working late) is not around to help calm her down. Such contextual relational issues are rarely included in observation codes. Unless the mother/father relational issue receives primary emphasis, the carefully described mother/child sequence will be resistant to change.

To reiterate, both diagnostic and home observational methods can provide necessary additional material for the therapist. However, since the information they provide is not of a relational nature, they must be used only when an understanding of family themes and functions has already been developed.

SUGGESTED READINGS

Bowen, M. *Family therapy in clinical practice.* New York: Aronson, 1978. *Family structural concepts such as fusion and differentiation, triangulation, and multigenerational transmission provide schematics that go beyond specific interactions for understanding families. Bowen is particularly sensitive to the interplay between the individual and larger family processes and structures.*

Haley, J. *Problem-solving therapy.* San Francisco: Jossey-Bass, 1976. *The major strength of this basic work is its clear and straightforward description of family change techniques. Although the book is rich in theory, the straightforward and practical style allows for easy translation into specific interventions.*

Minuchin, S. *Families and family therapy.* Cambridge, Mass.: Harvard University Press, 1974. *The written descriptions and visual schematics in this book provide an excellent model for conceptualizing family process and structure. Clear case illustrations and descriptions of techniques give readers numerous vehicles for creating family change.*

Patterson, G. R., & Reid, J. B. Reciprocity and coercion: Two facets of social systems. In C. Neuringer & G. L. Michael (Eds.), *Behavior modification in clinical psychology.* New York: Appleton-Century-Crofts, 1970. *This is a classic paper in the social-learning approach to family interaction. Reciprocity and coercion are not only a major and problematic interactional form but also a model for understanding discrete behavioral sequences in the context of larger functional outcomes.*

CHAPTER 3

Instituting Change: Therapy

With the assessment phase of intervention comes the phase we choose to call therapy. As indicated in the previous chapter, change really begins during the assessment phase, which is intermingled with therapy. For the sake of orderliness and ease of presentation, however, we present these phases here as sequential not simultaneous.

The therapy phase is designed to modify the cognitive sets, attitudes, expectations, labels, affective reactions, and assumptions of the family. When family members enter treatment, they usually have a range of explanations for their plight; these explanations generally include or imply a cognitive and affective component: "I get depressed because he cares more for his work than for me." "The kids act up because she undermines me." "The doctor said that setting fires gives him a sense of power." Embedded in almost all these explanations is the message "If you just change him (or her or me), things will get better." Family members arrive with an idea of who is "it"; they generally think of this identified patient as having something wrong with his or her motives, feelings, desires, or attitudes. The identified patient, in turn, usually cooperates in this labeling process by being defensive, weird, uncooperative, and otherwise unhelpful. All family therapists recognize the importance of shifting the focus from the

47

identified patient to the family relationships that create and maintain pathological behavior. The therapist must move the family members from an individualistic and singular-cause way of thinking to thinking about how relationships, not specific behaviors or feelings or thoughts, create problems. The therapist must help family members to see themselves and each other as recipients rather than malevolent causes and to recognize that there will be benefits for each of them in the change process.

To accomplish these ends, a goal in the early stages of therapy —contrary to popular opinion—is to move the family from certainty to confusion. For example, as long as family members "know" the problem is "caused" by the son's identity crisis, they can passively sit back (if the therapist is lucky) or actively resist (if the therapist is unlucky) until the son finds his identity. If the son lived in a vacuum, he could probably be helped to do so relatively easily. But finding an identity often takes years, if it happens at all, when other family members consistently counteract the process. The good sibling is lavishly reinforced for reporting the son's screw-ups; the father continues to give mixed messages by lecturing both about being able to stand on one's own feet and about the need to follow orders; and the mother continues alternatively to support her son and her husband.

Once they stop maintaining their image of the son as being "it," the family members can begin to question their causal interpretations, and change can begin. For example, if the son can be relabeled as the recipient of mixed messages from his parents as well as from his friends and the mass media, if the father can be relabeled as the lonely power figure who is uncertain and fearful of losing contact, and if the mother can be relabeled as the victim of her fear of losing one or more members of the family, then who was to blame and what is the problem? If the therapist can help the family members become uncertain that the problem resides in the identified patient, they can begin to examine the relationship patterns that ultimately produce the undesirable behavior. Because families rarely have or accept such a view of their relationships, functional family therapists have had to develop a set of techniques to help families see themselves and their relationships in this way. Acquiring this different perception is necessary if families are to become able and willing to benefit from the other major component of intervention, education.

In fact, the point of the therapy phase is to bring all family members to the point where they can benefit from the education we subsequently offer them. In different terms, therapy is designed to help them want to change; education provides them with the techniques for changing. Thus therapy tends to focus on their motivational states—feelings, cognitions, and the attributions they make about one another. Education, in contrast, tends to focus on changing overt behavior and problem-solving sequences.

Our aim in the therapy phase—especially in the first two sessions—is to have each family member leave with these thoughts and feelings:

1. The therapist "sided" with me as much as with the others.
2. The therapist helped me see how my behavior relates to everyone else's behavior.
3. The therapist made it clear that I am not to blame. Even though I contributed to the problem, I am as much a victim as is everyone else.
4. The therapist helped me see how everyone else is also a victim and a participant. I now see the rest of my family in a different light.
5. The therapist helped me see that our problem isn't what I thought it was. Whereas I used to think our problem resulted from different needs, goals, and the like, I now see that our problem resulted because we didn't know how to resolve our differences.
6. I feel that if we continue with the program I will be safer, happier, and better able to get what I want.

The reasons for moving family members to this attitudinal point are pragmatic. If they feel blamed, they will behave defensively. If they don't feel change will be better for them, they will resist. And—worst of all—if one or all of them refuse to come back for subsequent sessions, there are few (if any) ways the therapist can help them.

In order for every family member to emerge with the positive feelings and thoughts listed above, the therapist must utilize a number of specific techniques. In addition, the therapist must work (sometimes very hard) to develop and maintain a special attitude. Unless the therapist is a very good actress or actor, the therapist will have difficulty helping a father whom the therapist sees as malevolent, condescending, and uncaring to feel like a victim. Thus, in many ways the techniques described in this chapter are designed as much to help the therapist as to help the family. To the extent that therapists can utilize these techniques, they are less likely to blame, look for scapegoats, and lose their enthusiasm and hope for positive change.

As a final introductory note, we must emphasize that these techniques cannot be used in a vacuum. Instead, how they are used must be based on the assessment information (Chapter 2) that the therapist is simultaneously gathering. The functions of behavior, in particular, must be kept in mind as the therapist formulates what to say or do.

TECHNIQUES THAT DEVELOP
A FOCUS ON RELATIONSHIPS

The therapist (particularly in the early phases of interaction) does everything possible to identify behaviors, thoughts, and feelings and to help the family see how their behaviors, thoughts, and feelings interrelate. Techniques the therapist can use to achieve this new focus are discussed here. In all cases, the therapist avoids allowing the session to become focused on one or more of the family members as individuals. Doing so only allows family members to continue seeing the problem as being the fault of a particular individual.

In using these techniques, therapists need to maintain some degree of creativity and flexibility. We (and all other therapists we know) vary in how much and in what form we use various techniques to develop a focus on relationships. Some therapists move chairs around or reseat family members to accentuate certain relationships. Others use humor ("You mean all this misery is over garbage!"), and others touch family members. To the extent that therapists can develop a wide range of both explicit and implicit techniques, they have more options available as avenues to change. However, therapists must be cautioned against seeing these techniques as ends in themselves. The same techniques that work for a therapist with one family may be totally ineffective for a different therapist or family. The main point is to remember the goal of these techniques: to help families see themselves as a set of relationships, not as individuals who are bad, sick, crazy, or separate.

Asking Questions

At times such as early in the first session when the therapist has almost no information, questions become one of the main devices (if not the only one) for focusing on relationships. A short excerpt from the first session of Debbie's family demonstrates the use of questions to refocus on relationships.

> *Therapist:* The only information I received was that Debbie has been referred for being a runaway five times during the past three months. Debbie, can you tell me how you came to receive all this attention?
>
> (Debbie shrugs and looks down. There is an awkward—for the therapist at least—pause of ten seconds.)
>
> *Mother:* It's been comin' on for a year and a half now. She's been getting worse and worse 'til I just can't control her any more.
>
> *Therapist:* Control?
>
> *Mother:* Oh, you know, get her to listen. Any time I tell her to do something she gets that smart look on her face—like she's doin' now—and either walks away or says something smart mouth.
>
> *Therapist:* Dad—uh—do they call you Dad at home? (Father nods.) How do you fit into all this?
>
> *Father:* I—I get in when I get home. She's (gestures toward his wife) bouncin' off the walls, all agitated like, and as soon as I get in the door she starts in on me about how Debbie did this and Debbie didn't do that.

By asking Father about his role, the therapist diffuses the tendency for Mother to continue to focus on Debbie's misbehavior. Further, the therapist now has two sets of relationships on which to focus: Mother/Debbie and Mother/Father. This situation is far superior to one in which the therapist allows the focus to remain on the goodness or badness of any one person's behavior.

If, after Mother's description of what she meant by control, the therapist had asked "Why does this bother you so much?", the therapist would have added legitimacy to Mother's stance as a victim of Debbie's misbehavior and would have given her an opening for even more diatribes against Debbie. Then the therapist's task of relabeling Debbie as a victim would have been difficult. Or, if the therapist had asked Debbie "How do you feel about what your mother just said?", Debbie probably would have shrugged, merely solidifying her role as "it" and in turn producing such reactions from Mother as "Tell the man what you feel" or "See, she won't talk to you either."

The main point here is that families tend to focus on individuals and their badness, and therapists must help move them to a focus on relationships. Asking questions that facilitate blaming and attributing of negative labels is unnecessary and counterproductive. To avoid making change harder than it already is, the therapist must ask questions about relationships not about the "problem" people.

Making Comments

Simply commenting on the apparent impact of behavior and feelings can also help identify and clarify the relationships among family members. To return to the excerpt from Debbie's family:

> *Therapist* (to Father): So you get drawn into this when Mother gets upset about Debbie?
> *Father:* Yeah, and I'm tired of the whole thing.

Here the therapist has set the stage for several alternative maneuvers for refocusing on relationship issues. Rather than being locked into a focus on Debbie's badness, for example, the therapist can refocus on the impact of the Mother/Debbie relationship on the husband/wife relationship. In fact, the apparent problem of Debbie can begin to recede in emphasis, and the therapist can begin to help the family members see themselves as engaged in a set of interlocking and unhappy relationships in which all are suffering. If the refocusing is successful, all family members will be willing to invest in change.

Interrelating Feelings, Thoughts, and Behavior

The previous excerpt already demonstrated this technique somewhat; the therapist related Father's being drawn in to Mother's feeling upset. In a different case a therapist might say "So when your husband *behaves* that way, you *interpret* it as his not loving you, and you *feel* rejected." Or "Oh, so when your dad becomes *upset* you find some 'legitimate' place like the library to *go* to. That way the issue between you two cannot be resolved directly." Or "If I'm hearing you right it's when you *feel* overwhelmed that you *send* the kids to Grandma's."

In all these examples, no one person is seen as pivotal, causal, or bad. Instead, they are each seen as responding to the constraints placed by others as well as simultaneously placing constraints. Like the chicken and egg, neither comes first. Instead they both result from and cause the other. As family members begin to see themselves in this light, they become less vested in proving that others are bad and become more willing to engage in the educational techniques of change that will help them all emerge from the quagmire of blaming, coercion, and defensiveness in which they are caught.

Offering Interpretations

The boundary separating the areas of interpretation from comments and even leading questions is murky and probably inconsequential. We think of interpretations as involving more inference and guesswork than do comments. To return to a previous example and carry it further, a therapist says to a divorced mother "If I'm hearing you right, it's when you feel overwhelmed that you send the kids to Grandma's." Then the therapist says to Grandma "So whenever the kids come over you know it is a signal that your daughter feels overwhelmed?" Grandma nods. The therapist says to Mother "Did Grandma give you the message that the kids should be emissaries, or did you figure this out on your own, for fear that you couldn't ask her for help directly?" Here the therapist is doing some guessing (interpreting) about the causes and payoffs (the function) of the relationship. The therapist is hypothesizing that one function of Mother's ineptness with her kids is that it allows her to receive some nurturance from her own mother. Because Grandma feels Mother had made her own decisions by having the children and getting a divorce and now has to live with these decisions, she won't offer support if Mother asks for it overtly. However, she can't refuse to help when the situation is bad for her grandchildren, whom she doesn't feel are responsible. The kids have, in a sense, been made into pawns in the ambivalent and coercive relationship that exists between their mother and their grandmother.

Interpretations thus go beyond the obvious content and involve inferring motivational states, long-term impacts, and historical antecedents. Because they go beyond the obvious, they can be quite powerful in moving the family rapidly through the therapy phase. Unfortunately, they also have great potential for being off the mark, particularly when therapists involve their own projections and value systems. Thus interpretations should probably be used sparingly at first; as therapists become experienced and develop a feel for families, they can use them to a greater extent, thus speeding up the process of therapy.

Identifying Sequences

The identification of sequences of behavior is an effective technique for teasing out the relational picture in family interaction. It is particularly useful when families are naturally straightforward and concrete and when they tend to become involved in rapid chains of interaction. Sequencing slows the pace of these interactions, helping the therapist to make explicit what was previously implicit (Madanes, 1980) and helping the family members to see these interactions as understandable and potentially controllable.

Consider a family referred for the daughter's truancy and repeated curfew violations. During the first session, the parents and Suzy discuss the most recent occasion of Suzy's coming home well after curfew. The therapist then says: "Now before we go on I want to make sure I have this right. Mom and Dad were watching TV discussing what to do when Suzy got home. Dad asked Mom to stay out of it because she tended to become so upset, and he thought he could handle it better. Mom agreed and went to the bedroom. Suzy came home and went straight for her room. Dad, you sort of chased her and said—nicely—'We need to talk about this.' Suzy, you turned to continue to your room and Dad grabbed your arm and swung you around. You then tried to pull away saying 'Leave me alone.' At this point, Mom, you came out of the bedroom and said something like 'Don't let her just go in there and hide from this.'"

By sequencing the events to this point the therapist has complete control of the family's relational picture. The therapist can emphasize certain aspects of the picture and deemphasize others. In this instance, he decides to switch away from Suzy as the curfew violator and to focus instead on the husband/wife relationship. To accomplish this shift in focus, the therapist offers an interpretation.

> *Therapist:* Okay, before I finish the sequence of events, I must check something out. Mom, by coming out at this point, it could seem that you didn't believe your husband could take care of the situation as he promised. Did you intend to send him that message?
>
> *Mother:* Oh, no, I just heard her start going into her routine, and I. . . .
>
> *Therapist* (interrupting): Okay, but let's check this out. (To Father:) Did you feel this way, or am I way off here?

Father: Oh . . . no . . . I never guess I . . . I'm so used to her becoming upset. . . .

Therapist: That you don't really think of it in terms of her
protecting you.

Father: Protecting me?

Therapist: In a sense, yes. If you promise to take care of it,
and it starts becoming chaotic, and Mom then bombs in—
then we never really know if you can take care of the situation on your own . . . so it. . . .

Mother (interrupting): But I didn't mean to. . . .

Therapist (interrupting): Yeah, and that's what is the really
tough part. We do all kinds of things that send a bunch of
messages. Some we know we want to send, some we aren't
even aware of. Then things become habits—like in your
home we have the weekly Suzy curfew fights. (Shrugs with
a smile, the family chuckles.) Dad feels caught between you
two women. Suzy feels she can't begin to try to make her
own decisions without being outnumbered two to one, so
she starts to withdraw. And Mom is frightened about losing
control of her daughter. Now we can back up a bit and
begin, say, with you two. (Points at Mom and Dad.) Let's
see if we can begin to let each other know in new ways
what we want, need, and expect from each other.

Mother: But what about Suzy's . . . uh. . . .

Therapist: I appreciate your concern, and I promise Suzy
won't be left out in the cold. In fact, once you two learn
these new ways of sharing, then *you* can take more of the
responsibility for learning new ways to share with Suzy.
Okay?

Mother: Okay. (Father nods.)

A number of things occur in this extended vignette, some of which
we discuss later as we elaborate other techniques. For now we wish
to emphasize a progression of events. After the therapist identified
a behavioral sequence, he began hypothesizing several functional
relationships, emphasizing the interlocking nature of the family's
needs, impacts, and expectations. In doing so, the therapist shifted
the focus of intervention from the problem (curfew violation) to
the process used by the family members to resolve their troublesome relationships. Finally, the therapist began moving into the
educational phase of intervention (see the next chapter) by
indicating he would help the family learn new ways to interact.

Using the Therapist as a Direct Tool

In addition to using social and linguistic tools, therapists can use themselves in implicit and explicit ways to develop a focus on relationships. This technique involves making overt references to how the therapist interacts with a family: "So, Mrs. Davis, you felt things were so urgent you needed outside help, but you, Mr. Davis, didn't want to come to these sessions. It looks as though I'm in the position of backing you into a corner, Mr. Davis, being a man your wife has brought into the situation when you two couldn't resolve it between you. That is where the action is [pointing back and forth between them], and that is the first issue we must resolve." In this instance the therapist uses an overt reference to himself and to how Mrs. Davis might be using him to focus attention on the marriage relationship. Not coincidentally, this maneuver also goes a long way toward reducing Mr. Davis's defensiveness. By talking about the inherent coalition that exists between himself and the motivated family member, the therapist lessens the potency of that coalition and begins forming one with Mr. Davis.

Or, to return to the case of the divorced mother, the therapist might say: "It sounds like my advice might not be consistent with your mother's. Would following my advice represent a rejection by you of your mother?" The therapist could have included an interpretation, by adding that the mother seemed to set up her parent figures (her mother and the therapist) to disagree, just as children often do with their own parents. Instead he used the reference to the therapist/mother relationship to refocus on the mother/grandmother relationship. The therapist then suggested that grandmother attend the next session. This maneuver helps to move the mother out of her isolated-single-parent framework into a relational framework, which is both realistic and constructive.

Techniques for using the therapist implicitly as a tool include mood accentuation, humor, and nonverbal cueing. Transcript examples fail to capture the impact of such techniques. For example, a therapist might look increasingly sad as two people argue and finally announce: "Maybe I'm the only one that this means anything to, but you two are so busy attacking and defending that neither of you has given the other a chance to hear the pain and fear you have. Can you tell me, or each other, why sharing your pain is more dangerous than clobbering each other?" In this instance the therapist helps the couple shift their focus from the content of their argument to the process of communicating in their relationship.

For an example of nonverbal cueing consider this case. A mother characteristically launches into long monologues involving unnecessary detail. After failing to influence her style by using direct methods, the therapist adopts the head-down, staring-at-shoes position of her husband. After only ten seconds, the mother somewhat angrily responds.

Mother: Stop that. I know what you're trying to do.

Therapist: And it upset you.

Mother: Damn right. At least I'm trying. . . . I'm doin' the best I can.

Therapist: And my sitting like this doesn't give you much credit, does it?

Mother: No. (Begins to become teary eyed. Father furtively glances up.)

Therapist (to Father): I'm guessing now, but I'd guess that you've given up trying to outdo your wife because she's a pretty powerful talker. . . . (Father looks up more directly.) But while you thought you were protecting yourself, she felt "uncredited" and (looks at wife) probably pretty lonely.

The therapist at this point can move in several directions that were unavailable as long as the mother continued her usual monologues. In reaching this point, the therapist used several techniques but initiated the entire process by accentuating a nonverbal component of the marriage relationship.

Stopping and Starting Interaction

In the opening rounds of treatment it may be necessary to actively intervene and block a particular interaction. For example, a father prone to long monologues that document the total irresponsibility of his son might best be stopped from giving further examples: "Is this another example of how terrible your son has been acting? If it is, I want you to stop. I can appreciate your need to convince me, but at this point further information serves to anger and alienate Bill, something I don't think you want." Stopping interaction patterns induces stress and forces new lines of communication to develop. Once labeled from a functional point of view, transactions such as this one can be put into an entirely new perspective, the perspective of personal responsibility: "You have been giving a monologue again, Dad.

Knowing what effect it has on Bill, I have to assume that you are choosing to create distance between you and Bill here. And, Bill, you cooperate by dropping your head and staring at the floor. Is this what you two want?"

The purpose of starting interaction patterns in a family session is to develop relationships that have atrophied because of extensive rigidity. If a stepfather and daughter are not initiating contact with each other because the mother is overprotective of the daughter and reluctant to turn over control to her husband, it may be necessary to facilitate the stepfather/daughter relationship in order to initiate change. This procedure is particularly necessary if the stepfather is directed by the mother to enforce her rules and the daughter rebels. Blocking the mother's switchboard role while enabling interaction between the stepfather and daughter can provide excellent information about the husband/wife relationship while elevating the stepfather's position in the home. Starting interaction patterns requires that the therapist be competent to give directions in a clear and concise fashion. The therapist must not ask family members to do something but must tell them what to do. To be effective, the directions must also be based on a clear conceptualization of the family structure; in particular, they cannot violate the already established functions of family patterns.

TECHNIQUES THAT CHANGE MEANING

In addition to emphasizing the relational qualities of family interaction, the therapist must also help the family members interpret their relationships in a different light. Before the prognosis for intervention becomes good, all family members must adopt the specific set of attitudes listed in the beginning of this chapter. A series of techniques have been developed to facilitate the transition from skepticism, defensiveness, and resentment to hope and enthusiasm.

Nonblaming and Relabeling

Undoubtedly the most used and most influential techniques are nonblaming and relabeling. Nonblaming and relabeling help cast all family members in a benign light (Weakland et al., 1974; Soper & L'Abate, 1977) by modifying how family members think and feel about themselves and each other. Family members seem to be conceptually lazy when they have to explain emotion-arousing or unpredictable behavior (such as why adolescent children now hate their parents). They are more likely to make simplistic and parsimonious trait attributions ("He's a lazy, irresponsible brat") than to make situational and contextual analyses ("He seems to argue most frequently when he wants to assert himself and his mother and I either ignore him or clamp down on him"). One component of a therapist's relabeling efforts must therefore include introducing contextual focus that takes into account the interdependence of family members (Weakland, 1976).

This complex and inclusive focus not only reduces trait attributions but also reduces the perplexity and fear aroused in family members by each others' behavior. If the therapist can make behavior seem logical, adaptive, and legitimate, family members are likely to appreciate how they relate to each other. This appreciation can produce a nonthreatening environment for change; family members will not feel the need to defend themselves, nor will they find it necessary to be threatened or intimidated by each other (see also the concept of positive connation in Palazzoli-Selvini, Boscolo, Cecchin, & Prata, 1974).

The excerpt in which the therapist relabeled a mother as protective of the father illustrated the relabeling process. Alternative labels could have been generated, such as nagging, intrusive, castrating, or nosey. These labels, however, are pejorative and might have created defensiveness and additional blaming. Labeling the behavior as protective, however, allows it to be seen in a benign light. Then, in subsequent sessions the therapist can help the mother develop new ways to relate to, and even protect, the father. In this benign context, she is likely to be a willing participant in the process. Relabeling thus need not be accurate in the sense of describing the true motivational states of family members. Making family members aware of malevolent patterns and motivations, in fact, often generates increased resistance (Stanton, 1980b). Benign labels can produce enthusiasm for change.

Relabeling may take a somewhat different form.

Therapist (to Father): What do you want from these sessions?
Father: I want a third party to explain to Sharon the bad effects of drugs.
Therapist (to Mother): What would you like from these sessions?
Mother: I want to know and understand Sharon.

> *Therapist* (to Daughter): What do you want from these sessions?
> *Daughter* (with a shrug): I don't know.
> *Mother:* Is that a healthy attitude?
> *Therapist:* That's a good question, but I've got to answer you this way. It seems that you, Mother, and you, Father, want different things. So it seems Sharon may be just cooling it until she figures out what each of you wants.

This new label, admittedly somewhat forced, is designed to remove the "unhealthy" label from Sharon and to make her seem sensibly conservative in the light of contradictory messages. Note that Sharon herself contributes to her "unhealthy" label by being uncommunicative and sullen. Thus in this case the therapist has to talk for Sharon, who is in essence benignly relabeled despite herself.

Therapists must be careful to avoid relabeling in an arbitrary fashion. When a father expresses only intense anger toward his son, it is unlikely that relabeling him as a loving father will be acceptable to the family. To relabel him as frustrated because of his inability to control his son may be sufficiently plausible. This relabeling not only may have an impact on the father's image but may also make the son willing to negotiate with a father he sees as frustrated rather than as hateful. In a similar vein, all interventions must be tailored to "a given family's values, sociocultural context, and distinctive 'style'" (Stanton, 1980b, p. 377).

In some families, particularly those manifesting disturbed symptoms (for example, schizophrenia) or those in which one member has strong extratherapeutic ties that counteract change (a stable extramarital affair, a smothering grandmother), relabeling techniques may encounter consistent resistance. This resistance takes one of two forms: refusing to accept the new label ("But if she weren't sick she wouldn't become confused") or jumping from topic to topic and innuendo to innuendo so the therapist cannot isolate a manageable theme to question, interpret, identify sequences in, or relabel. In such cases the therapist must sometimes utilize alternative techniques to create the attitudinal context for change.

Overtly Discussing the Implications of Symptom Removal

What would the implications be for a family if the depressed husband became less depressed? Would the change in the relationship between husband and wife be unbearable if he were to get well? What consequences are there for a family if the kids are no longer a problem? Would the marital conflict be highlighted? By asking such questions directly the therapist confronts family members and forces them to consider how the family's situation would be threatened if the presenting symptoms were removed. In doing so, the therapist does not immediately challenge the family's notion about what the problem is. Rather, the therapist requires the family members to deal directly with the identified patient in the area of the symptom. This technique may take the form also, for example, of a simple warning to the parents that they may not be able to handle the consequences to themselves if their habitually truant child were to become symptom free by suddenly attending school.

Changing the Impact or Context of the Symptom

In a related vein, therapists occasionally must exaggerate the symptom so that it no longer serves the functions it previously did. In a family with a young fire setter the therapist instructs both parents to monitor a program that requires the youngster to light matches at the sink and extinguish them in water. This program, which lasts for 30 minutes each evening for a week, creates shared parenting and intensifies discussion about the behavior within the family. Certain patterns are changed. The sequence of fire setting, Mother's subsequent hysteria, and punitive action by Father on arriving home is replaced by education, monitoring, and competent parenting. Instructing an adolescent identified as a chronic shoplifter to steal from his father without getting caught is another example of intensifying the symptom in order to force family members to regulate it (Minuchin, 1974).

Shifting the Focus from One Problem or Person to Another

A single mother of two hyperactive children, ages 3 and 5, initiates therapy to stop her younger son's temper tantrums. In the first session the therapist hypothesizes that the relational impact of the temper tantrums is the loss of private time and freedom for the mother because of the increased contact she must have with the child. The therapist tells the mother that he can teach her how to eliminate the tantrums and that he can also help her work on her feelings of being trapped and isolated. He thus redefines the problem as centering around her adjustment to single life, the unresolved issues from her marriage, and her general fears regarding intimacy. By defusing the tantrums as a focus the therapist is able to move to central issues within the family: the child's sense of abandonment if he becomes symptom free, and the mother's use of the child as a legitimate reason to stay home.

Because of the relational impact of symptoms it is also possible to move the therapeutic focus from one family member to another. A family is referred for therapy because the 15-year-old son has been arrested for exposing himself in the park. During the initial stages of treatment the father begins to stutter as he discusses his early problems with dating. He admits to being quite anxious about his son's behavior. As the therapist begins to probe, the father says that he had severe speech problems while dating as a teenager but is surprised that he is stuttering currently because it has not been a problem for many years. The mother further reveals that since their marriage her husband has become quite a public speaker and that she had all but forgotten that her husband used to have a stuttering problem. So as not to intimidate the son, the therapist moves to the new problem of stuttering by encouraging both parents to discuss how they dealt with the stuttering problem; the therapist thus attempts to address the issue of parental unrest regarding the son's emerging sexuality. The therapist can now move, during the course of treatment, back and forth between these problems, while beginning to develop strategies for the parents to use to monitor and regulate their son's acting out.

TECHNIQUES THAT ENCOURAGE MOVING FROM THERAPY TO EDUCATION

Dealing with Resistance

We have listed numerous techniques for successfully intervening therapeutically with families. Unfortunately, these techniques are not always immediately successful. As we discussed previously, one or more family members may demonstrate resistance, which indicates that they do not as yet accept the idea that the change will be beneficial for them. Resistance takes many forms, including (1) not accepting a new label ("What do you mean 'protecting' me? I don't need her protection"), (2) not accepting a refocusing on relationships ("You make it sound like we're confusing her. We communicate the same thing. She just doesn't listen"), (3) continuing to give long monologues that emphasize a particular person's badness ("But if she wouldn't be so smart ass. I mean like the other night she . . . she was unbelievable. She came home late to begin with. Then when I asked her where she had been she started smarting off. Then all I did was . . . ''), (4) becoming hysterical or otherwise overwhelmed with emotion ("But [begins to cry], but . . . oh, I don't know how to . . . it's all just so . . . unnecessary [head down, crying] ''), (5) directly questioning the therapist's expertise ("It might look that way to you, but . . . well, I don't know how to say this, but you look kind of young. Do you have teenagers of your own?").

In responding to these forms of resistance, therapists must remember to retain their relational and nonblaming attitude and to avoid becoming defensive, angry, or impatient. They must realize that their comments or new labels are simply not appropriate for this family at this time, and they must formulate new ones. Therapists can respond to these statements of resistance in a nonblaming, relational way: (1) "I'm sure you're right. What is your word for what happens when she becomes upset and intervenes before you can handle it yourself?" (2) "And how do you two help each other deal with it when you think she's not listening?" (3) "It sounds like you feel pretty frustrated by this, Mom. Dad, have you been able to think of ways that will help Mom feel less frustrated?" (4) "Suzie, what is the impact on you when your mother expresses hopelessness like she's feeling now?" (5) "No, you're right. Just as your son has never been a father, you've never been a mother, and so on. None of us has ever really experienced what the other has, and that's why we're working so hard to help each other understand."

These responses may also meet resistance, which is why the early phases of therapy seem like a search for the most useful way to refocus and relabel. If the therapist's responses are relational and nonblaming, however, family members will probably be tolerant as the therapist searches for an approach that will begin to help them change their attitudinal set.

Introducing Education

While making the therapeutic maneuvers described above, the therapist looks for cues that the family is ready for the introduction of educational techniques. The resistance cues described above indicate the family is not yet ready. Acceptance of refocusing and of nonblaming relabeling maneuvers, however, indicates that the therapist should immediately institute an educational change program.

Acceptance is sometimes indicated by overt cues such as verbal agreement and nodding. Other times it is reflected in comments or questions that indicate acceptance of the therapist's refocusing implicitly. To return to an earlier example:

Father: It might look that way to you, but . . . well, I don't know how to say this, but you look kind of young. Do you have teenagers of your own?

Therapist: No, you're right. Just as your son has never been a father, you've never been a mother, and so on. None of us has ever really experienced what the other has, and that's why we're working so hard to help each other understand.

Father: But how can we understand?

Therapist: We can begin by learning to tell each other about ourselves in different ways. Let's begin with. . . . (Begins a communication-training exercise.)

Finally, acceptance is sometimes reflected in silence. Often after a therapist focuses on relationships and relabels, the family doesn't know what to say. Because the refocusing is plausible, they cannot contradict it. And because it does not blame anyone, they cannot resist. In such instances, family members simply have a "Well, go on" look on their faces. In response, the therapist should shift to education: "So, we see the issue, but we don't have a way right now for these things to work more happily for you. Let's begin to move in that direction by trying [an educational technique]."

In the next chapter, we describe in detail educational techniques that can follow successful therapy.

SUGGESTED READINGS

Beier, E. G. *The silent language of psychotherapy*. Chicago: Aldine-Atherton, 1966. *One of the earliest descriptions of communication-theory principles, this straightforward book is written from the therapist's perspective. It provides concepts and techniques that can free the therapist from many natural, but countertherapeutic, responses.*

Haley, J. *Strategies of psychotherapy*. New York: Grune & Stratton, 1963. *Considered by many to be the bible of systems approaches to family therapy, this book provides a clear conceptual underpinning for intervention techniques with individuals, couples, and families.*

Haley, J. *Problem-solving therapy*. San Francisco: Jossey-Bass, 1976. *The major strength of this basic work is its clear and straightforward description of family change techniques. Although the book is rich in theory, the straightforward and practical style allows for easy translation into specific interventions.*

Minuchin, S. *Families and family therapy*. Cambridge, Mass.: Harvard University Press, 1974. *The written descriptions and visual schematics in this book provide an excellent model for conceptualizing family process and structure. Clear case illustrations and descriptions of techniques give readers numerous vehicles for creating changes in families.*

Satir, V. *Conjoint family therapy*. (Rev. ed.). Palo Alto, Calif.: Science and Behavior Books, 1967. *A classic in the family therapy field, this early work demonstrates how systems and communication concepts can be translated into clear and well-described techniques.*

CHAPTER 4

Maintaining Change: Education

Education in functional family therapy is the process of providing a context for people to learn specific skills that they can use to maintain positive change. Therapy doesn't help people learn new skills; it merely helps people become receptive to learning them. And therapy, without specific skill training, leaves families almost at the mercy of luck to find specific new ways to interact. For example, a mother may come to realize in the therapy phase that her nagging no longer elicits cooperation and has in fact come to elicit active avoidance. But unless the therapist can help her in carefully planning a new way of behaving, she may be worse off than before aware of her part in the maladaptive process yet totally unable to respond effectively. In fact, suicide attempts, drug ingestions, divorces, and the like are not uncommon outcomes of therapy. Although such outcomes can conceivably be seen as positive in that they reflect growth, they can be avoided by providing sufficient education so that people can interact adaptively and in ways that make them happier. Therapy without education is unfocused, arbitrary, and inefficient; the positive changes and attributions that are produced in therapy will not be maintained unless people experience environmental behavior changes that support these new attributions. In maladaptive families, these environmental behavior changes can be developed and maintained through carefully planned educational activities. It must be remembered, however, that therapeutic intervention cannot begin with the educational phase. Clients often refuse to accept educational attempts until therapists have effectively accomplished therapy—until they have modified the family's expectations, attributions, labels.

Keeping in mind that successful education is based on successful therapy, the therapist offers educational techniques in two steps: rationale (goals) and specific operations. A rationale is given so that the family can see how a particular technique will deal with an issue they feel is important. The rationale that is presented to the family need not always be entirely "true," but it must make sense from the family's frame of reference (Zuk, 1978). To return to the example of Debbie's family, one technique was having Mother complete an extensive chart daily. This chart included all the tasks that each child should have accomplished. At the end of the day, Mother turned the chart over to Father, who then made decisions (to be carried out by Mother) about allowances, curfew times, and the like. In this instance the therapist gave the rationale that although Mother was home to do the monitoring, she needed help from Father in making decisions (a rationale in keeping with the family's traditionalist philosophy). The therapist did not say to the family that the technique was designed to minimize the direct contact of Father and the children. (It had been hypothesized that in this family Father's avoidance behavior functioned to give him distance from and low contact with the children.) The plan allowed Father his separating function (he could read a chart rather than interact with the children directly), while at the same time allowing Mother her merging function (she could carry out decisions and thus legitimize her mothering role). This part of the rationale was not presented to the family because it would have embarrassed them or caused defensiveness. However, it does reflect how the assessment information, particularly the identification of functions, was translated into a particular educational technique.

The rationale that is provided depends on the value system and expectations of the family. For example, a husband who is proud of being part of a liberated couple might be told that communication training will help the couple share equally, while a husband in a traditional marriage in which both partners want him to be the boss might be told that communication training will help him receive the information needed to make good decisions.

The specific educational programs utilized can be placed in one of three distinct categories. The first category includes the operations commonly referred to in the literature as communication skills or negotiating. The second category comprises what might be called technical aids. In this group are specific behavioral programs such as time-out procedures, reminder cards, recording charts, and contingency contracting. The third category is interpersonal tasks—the therapist-directed activities designed to enhance communication, family structure, and the adaptive attainment of family functions.

COMMUNICATION SKILLS

Communication skills are procedures therapists implement to facilitate the congruent expression of feelings, thoughts, ideas, desires, and needs by family members. Clarifying both verbal and nonverbal messages is a key to helping the system become the solution. Much depends on how well therapists shape, model, and facilitate congruent communication patterns (Stuart & Lott, 1972). How people talk to one another, not necessarily what they say, determines the quality of relationships. Good communication includes being clear and direct, hearing the other person, taking responsibility for what is said and how it is said, discussing desires and the alternative ways desires can be achieved, and clarifying the impact of behaviors. Training family members in effective communication styles enables them to develop congruent transactions with each other.

An effective negotiation style is a general goal for all families because it provides an effective process by which they can resolve problematic issues. To give a simple example, a father and mother may be helped to resolve a curfew issue with their 16-year-old. The issue becomes less relevant a year or two later as the adolescent matures, but the way in which they resolve similar issues will be relevant as long as they have a relationship with each other. Successful negotiation requires brevity, source responsibility, directness, presentation of alternatives, congruence, concreteness, behavioral specificity, feedback, active listening (Alexander, 1974), and impact statements. In this section, each of these elements is briefly described.

Brevity

Communication must be short to avoid overwhelming the listener with too much information. In therapy family members are often asked to state their needs or reactions in ten or fewer words. The requirement reduces the number of unnecessary statements and the opportunity to blame others or make provocative accusations. By saying "I want you to help around the house" instead of "You never do anything around here except come home and read the paper; and, if you think the lawn stops growing just because you're at work, you're crazy," a wife reduces defensiveness in her husband and increases the possibility for change. An effective therapist can quickly seize on the idea that mowing the lawn and doing some evening chores will provide the husband with distance and private time while giving the wife necessary help, thus bringing desired change without disrupting the functions that regulate intimacy levels.

Source Responsibility

Needs and reactions should be expressed in "I" statements, which facilitate centering responsibility on the speaker. Family members are helped to avoid "non-I" statements such as "In this house . . . ," "Kids shouldn't . . . ," "It's not right for you to . . . ," and "It would be nice if . . . ." Instead, family members are taught to say "I want . . . ," "When the dishes aren't done, I feel. . . . " Keeping statements at a personal level reduces blaming and defensiveness.

Directness

Directness is the complement of source responsibility. By using "you" statements, the speaker avoids third-person comments, innuendoes, and inappropriate generalizations. Instead of making "non-you" statements such as "No one around here . . ." "If only someone would . . . ," "The atmosphere around here is . . . ," and (in front of husband) "He never . . . ," family members are encouraged to directly say "I don't want you to . . ." or "You are not to . . . ."

Presentation of Alternatives

By presenting alternatives, the speaker moves away from making nonnegotiable demands; all family members can benefit from being flexible in their problem-solving attempts. "How about your coming home every night at 8:30, or you can come home four nights at 8:00 and stay out one night until 10:30." Presenting alternatives transmits the message "We can solve this" rather than "You must solve this for me." They allow the speaker to retain a sense of control, yet also provide the listener with a sense of having options.

Congruence

Family members can be helped to present messages that are congruent, or consistent, at the verbal, nonverbal, and contextual levels. For example, a husband should tell his wife in a friendly manner that he wants her to spend more time with him, and he must make her spending more time with him contextually possible by being available. Family members can be shaped by the therapist to provide congruent verbal and nonverbal cues and can then be taught how to help each other to do so in the absence of the therapist.

Concreteness and Behavioral Specificity

Abstractions such as "being responsible" must be translated into specific behaviors to be performed at specific times. When trust is only emerging (or is still not present) an ambiguous situation provides too many opportunities for failure. A therapist can help family members translate their feelings and demands into specifics.

Feedback

Extensive research (for example, Parsons & Alexander, 1973) has demonstrated that in adaptive families members often interrupt each other to ask for clarification and to provide feedback. This feedback allows family members to understand each other. An excerpt from a family moving successfully toward termination demonstrates this process. The family is discussing the daughter's desire to go to a party.

Daughter: But everyone's going.
Mother: That's fine. I'm willing for you to go, but I need to have you home by 11:30. [Source responsibility and directness.]
Daughter: But sometimes getting the rides all arranged takes a long time, and. . . .
Mother (interrupting): Okay, just call me at 11:00 and tell me. . . .

Daughter (interrupting to give feedback): There's no phone in the cabin. (Pause; everyone seems to be thinking.)

Father: How 'bout you call from the pay phone at the grocery store before you drive up the canyon? [Brevity and behavioral specificity.] You can already have rides home arranged, and you can tell us who is driving you. [Presentation of alternatives.]

Daughter: Aw, that'll look like. . . .

Father (interrupting, brisk but not hostile): Hey, I realize that may be a bit awkward. But all the kids know we're having trouble, and they also know we wouldn't have even agreed for you to go if we hadn't been making progress here. I'm sorry if it embarrasses you, but it's the only way I can figure out for you to go—which is important for you—and for us to know what's going on—which is important to us. [Active listening, source responsibility, directness, impact statements—see below.] (Pause; good eye contact among all three.)

Daughter: Yeah . . . Okay. . . . You'll lend me the dime?

Father: Oh, Christ! (All laugh.)

Impact Statements

Impact statements provide personal reactions that require no justification from the speaker or listener. Their expression helps family members break up established associations between feelings and behavior. "When you do . . . , the effect on me is. . . ." "The impact on me when you . . . is that I feel. . . ."

Active Listening

Active listening (Rogers & Farson, 1957) is the presentation of cues by the listener both during the time when and after someone else communicates. These cues indicate accurate listening and include maintaining eye contact, nodding, leaning forward, and restating or rephrasing the content and the feelings communicated. Good listening is not an innate skill, however, as the following transcript demonstrates. In this case a young couple with two children from the wife's previous marriage is contemplating divorce after one and a half years of marriage. In the first session the therapist suggested that they had a poor process for talking to each other and therefore any decision they made would not be a good one. They agreed not to make any dramatic decisions until they felt capable of talking to one another effectively. The transcript begins near the end of the second session, after the couple has agreed to start some communication training.

Therapist: Why don't you start, Mark. What is it that you want from your wife?

Mark: I'm not sure what you mean . . . what do I want from . . . her. . . . Okay, let's see. I guess I want her to put me first, above everything. . . .

Therapist (interrupting): Can you talk directly to her about this? [Source responsibility, directness.]

Mark: I want you to put me first above everything. I'm tired of taking a back seat to your damn dogs and the kids. It seems that every time. . . .

Therapist (interrupting): Hold on a second. Let's not confuse things by getting her defensive. Try this: "What I want is . . . and the impact on me when I don't get it is that I feel. . . ."[Models concreteness, source responsibility, making an impact statement, and giving feedback.]

Mark: Okay. What I want is. . . . (To therapist:) Now I know what it is. . . . What I want is more time with you (looks at wife), and when I don't get it the impact on me is . . . I feel neglected. [Brevity, directness, source responsibility, congruence.]

Therapist: Good. Would it also be true for you to say that being neglected is like a personal rejection, and that hurts?

Mark: Yes, I often feel rejected. [Source responsibility, impact statement.]

Therapist: Susan, what did you hear out of all that? [Request for active listening.]

Susan: You know that really makes me mad. He wants me to have a hobby and stay home with the kids . . . and you know, uh, well, I just don't know what he wants, it seems to me that. . . . [Impact statement followed by long explanation that is not brief or concrete.]

Therapist: Before we get into what issues you have with him, I'd like you to repeat back what you heard him say. [Request for feedback and active listening.]

Susan: I can't remember.

Therapist: That's okay. It's hard to listen when you want to make a point. Mark, repeat what you just told Susan.

Mark: I want more time with you, and when I don't get it I feel rejected. [Brevity, source responsibility, directness.]

Therapist: Susan, I want you to repeat back to Mark what he just said to you. [Request for active listening.]

Susan (turning to Mark): You want more time with me, and when I am too busy you feel left out. [Active listening.]

Therapist: Good. Now, let's reverse this. Susan, what is it that you want from Mark?

Susan: I don't know. I haven't really thought about it.

Therapist (to both): You know, an important part of any love relationship is being able to look after one another. Knowing what your partner needs makes it easier to do that. It's hard to care for somebody if you don't know whether to leave him alone or give him a hug. . . . [Restatement of rationale.]

Therapist (to Mark, taking the pressure off Susan): You want time with your wife. If you are available and she can give it to you, great. [Bid for congruence.]

Therapist (to Susan): Let's try again. What is it that you want from Mark?

Susan: Well, uh, it's kind of hard to say. I'd like, you know, more contact, or, oh, something, after the kids are in bed. [Source responsibility, but somewhat ambiguous content.]

Therapist: You want a better sex life? [Request for concreteness.]

Susan: Not better. . . . I'd just like to have one! (Laughs nervously.) [Source responsibility, but still not direct.]

Therapist: By not having one, what impact does that have on you? [Request for impact statement.]

Susan: The impact on me is that I feel he doesn't love me and that maybe he's not attracted to me any more. [Source responsibility, impact statement.]

Therapist: Can you say that to him? [Request for directness.]

Susan: Since we've stopped making love, I feel that you don't want me and maybe that I'm not attractive to you any more. [Source responsibility, but the statement attributes motives, which is potentially destructive.]

Therapist: Stay with "I" statements—"I don't feel attractive any more. . . ."

Susan: . . . and I don't feel attractive any more.

Mark: Can I answer that?

Therapist: I don't think you need my permission, but first repeat back what she has said. [Request for active listening and feedback.]

Mark: You don't think I want to have sex with you and you feel either unloved or unattractive. . . . Uh, well . . . it's not that I don't love you or don't find you attractive. I do. It's just that, uh, I don't know, sometimes you don't seem to want to make love, being tired and all. . . . [Active listening, source responsibility, directness. Note that by saying "You don't seem" he is moving away from directly imputing motives to describing how the behavior implies a motive.]

Therapist: Are you angry with her for being tired and spending all her time with the dogs and kids? [This is a request for congruence because angry nonverbal cues are being sent.]

Mark: Yes, sometimes I feel very angry. [Source responsibility, brevity.]

Therapist: It seems to me that the two of you are very lucky in that you both want more contact. [Emphasizes the relationship; makes a positive statement.] Mark, you want more time, to be more central to her, and you, Susan, want some love and affection from him. I want you two to discuss this right now and stay on a personal level, don't bring in other issues like jobs, kids, and dogs. Also try to restate what has been said to you before answering.

Susan: A lot of things do seem to get in the way, but I'd like to get this straightened out. What do you mean by time? [Request for clarification; concreteness and specificity.]

Mark: I'd like to go out once in a while and know that you'd want to be with me.

Susan: You want to go out and know that I was there because I wanted to be. [Rephrasing.] Isn't being there enough? [Request for clarification.]

Mark: No, sometimes you . . . excuse me . . . I feel you're preoccupied with the other things, and. . . . [Congruence, source responsibility.]

Susan: You feel that I'm preoccupied with other things. [Active listening.] If I made the arrangements would that do it? [Presentation of alternatives.]

Mark: Yes, I'd love that. [Brevity, source responsibility, impact statement.]

Therapist: You two are doing good. What about this sex thing?

Mark: Hey, if we get to spend some time together. . . .

Therapist: Mark, talk to Susan.

Mark: After we go out or have some time to ourselves I just don't see it as being a problem. I really do find you attractive, and if I feel wanted I know we can work that out. In fact, I'm looking forward to getting home tonight. [Source responsibility.]

Therapist: We have a nice beginning here. I want to pursue this in our next session. As part of your homework assignment I want you to independently try and specify what it is you want from your partner. I want to see you in two days in order to capitalize on this nice beginning you two have worked so hard to get. [Assigning tasks, which gives responsibility for change to the couple.]

TECHNICAL AIDS

During the course of intervention many situations arise that require the therapist to use clear structural props for facilitating change. Although not meant to be a comprehensive inventory, the following list includes technical aids (or props) that have demonstrated such utility. The procedures are, by and large, products of the research into and the application of the social-learning model; they are all frequently cited in respected journals. They are not merely aids to treatment but powerful independent variables that are capable of permanently changing a variety of behaviors and processes. To the beginning family therapist having such a readily available armamentarium may be seductive and at times disruptive. It is not uncommon for a therapy session to change from a productive process to a mare's-nest because of the sudden introduction of a technical aid by an aspiring young therapist who is not giving proper attention to family process. If the context of behavior and the function it serves are not taken into account, the application of technical aids may seem capricious and insensitive to the struggling family. With this note of caution, we can discuss the legitimate use of technical aids in family therapy—what they are, how they are used, and what they can do.

Contingency Contracting

Contingency contracting is neither a new nor highly technical procedure. Bargaining is a form of conflict resolution that is probably as old as humanity. The field of mental health rediscovered the notion of striking a bargain and called it contingency contracting (Stuart, 1971; Tharp & Wetzel, 1969). Contracting should not be thought of as a situation in which each party gives up something. Instead, it is a process of bargaining in which all members receive something they want.

In a frequently encountered situation in problem families the parents want their son to do something that he is not doing (clean his room, wash the dishes), and the child wants his parents to do something that they are not doing (let him stay up until a certain hour). The therapist familiar with contingency contracting has a deceptively simple solution to such a problem: trade. The child agrees to wash the dishes, giving the parents what they want, and in turn the parents agree to let the child stay up later, thus giving him what he wants. Such everybody-wins solutions are the ideal in contingency contracting.

Good contracts require certain ingredients. Contracts must be *specific* regarding the gains each party expects as well as the responsibilities necessary to secure these gains. These responsibilities must also be *capable of being monitored*. Responsibilities that cannot be verified are beyond the scope of a contract, as they place heavy demands on trust. Although trust is an important ingredient in the functioning of adaptive families, it places too much strain on maladaptive families who are learning a new style of interaction. Contracts must also be *reasonable*. Initially we suggest that contracting not be undertaken with the mastery model in mind. Expecting 100% attendance at the outset from a previously truant youth may be an unrealistic goal. The national attendance rate for high school is roughly 80%, so why not four out of five days to begin with? By working in small steps families increase their chances of experiencing success (Weakland et al., 1974). Finally, contracts should be *open to change*. A discussion can enable the participants to evaluate, amend, terminate, or extend the agreement. In this way families can adjust to new data and make substantial strides toward becoming self-regulating.

Contingency contracting appears to be a particularly effective technique (1) when the problem is urgent and there is a need for the family to have a tool to work with immediately, (2) when there are faulty communication and negotiation styles, (3) when the problems are specific and behavioral (failing to go to school) rather than amorphous and attitudinal (not enjoying each other's company), (4) when parents have and are willing to apply control over the child and when they possess something the child wants. In addition, dictatorial and rigidly authoritarian parents are poor candidates for contracting because they cannot conceive of relinquishing absolute power. In this circumstance, more extreme therapeutic, rather than educational, techniques are required. Finally, contracting procedures have value to the extent that they are presented as problem-solving tools, generalizable to other situations, and as the first step in strengthening family communication patterns. (Readers interested in more complete descriptions of contingency contracting are urged to examine the excellent works of Stuart, 1971, and Stuart & Lott, 1972.)

Token Economies

Tokens, chits, points, and walking around money (WAMs) are essentially secondary reinforcers that are dispensed after the completion of a clearly specified behavior or behaviors. Family members can accumulate tokens, chits, points, or WAMs and then turn them in or use them for predetermined rewards. This clear exchange of reinforcing consequences for specified behaviors usually meets with the best results when used with young children and with quite concrete families. (For descriptions of token systems, see Allyon & Azrin, 1968, and Phillips, 1968.) Adolescents and noninstitutionalized adults are often less interested in such props and prefer clear verbal contracts.

In developing token or other reward systems it is necessary to determine whether the behavior targeted for change is part of the regulatory functions in the family and whether the change will be maintained as the technical aids are faded out. If, for example, a 9-year-old boy receives a token (which can then be exchanged for dessert and television privileges) from his mother for each 30-minute interval of nondisruptive behavior between the end of school and dinner time, problems will occur if compliance disrupts the separating function for the father, who has the mother's grudging permission to go out at night as long as everything is all right at the house. Shaping the son to be compliant will fail if the son's acting up is the only excuse the mother has to keep her husband from going out after dinner. Imagine the mother's position when she hears "You've done a great job with Billy; looks like everything is under control. See you later tonight; I'm going back to the office." How committed will the mother be to a program of watching timers, dispensing tokens, making desserts, and watching Walt Disney cartoons with Billy after discovering that the net result is less contact with her husband? Unraveling this interaction and developing alternative methods for maintaining the husband/wife functions must take priority over extinguishing the son's behavior.

The Three-Bell System and the Infraction System

Any family change program must include steps to be taken when a family member doesn't follow through. Families must learn to establish reasonable consequences for violations. One method particularly useful is the three-bell system. Essentially it follows the generally accepted practice in team sports. Players are not expected to play perfectly at all times. In baseball a batter can still attempt to hit the ball with a two-strike count; a college basketball player can still play with four fouls. But a third strike or a fifth foul means the player is sitting not playing. So, too, with families. If a person receives two warnings within a prescribed time period and nothing happens, the person picks up a third foul and must pay the piper. The usual consequences for adolescents and young children are room restriction, house restriction for short periods of time, additional chores, or restitution (which includes such acts as replacing broken items and cleaning up when messes are made).

In families that require extensive technical aids to deal with lack of compliance, an infraction system must occasionally be added. In this system three violations combine to constitute an infraction. Incurring a specified number of infractions during a specified time results in the loss of important privileges such as going out at night or having friends over. Also counted as infractions are violations of major limits or house rules that must be dealt with immediately. Not going to school is an example of a major violation of a house rule and requires immediate measures; using a three-bell system in this case would allow for too many missed school days.

In both these systems for dealing with noncompliance, it is always necessary that directives be clear, concise, and free of covert loopholes. (For interested readers an excellent source on this subject is Wood & Schwartz, 1977.)

Time-Out Strategies

Time-out strategies are important technical aids during the education phase. Simply stated, time-out procedures require removing an individual from a situation that maintains the undesired behavior or that provides other reinforcing consequences. When a young child has a tantrum, for example, it can be nicely handled by physically taking the child out of the immediate surroundings and placing him or her in a solitary and secluded place until the tantrum ends. Time-out procedures are simple, straightforward, and quickly reduce the frequency, duration, and intensity of high-rate and undesirable behaviors.

Teaching parents to use this procedure requires their mutual cooperation as well as commitment to the program—that is, therapy must be accomplished first. A time-out strategy must be agreed to by both parents; the one on the scene should carry it out with the other parent lending support. An underlying belief here is that children do not become problematic if parents are mutually supportive and contain their own conflict in the husband/wife arena.

Charts and Graphs

Educational aids of this type are generally used to maintain and reinforce acceptable or desired behavior. (A good primer on this subject is the workbook by Patterson & Gullion, 1971.) Family members define the desired behaviors they want from each other and document the occurrence of these behaviors on a prominent chart or graph. Levels of performance are monitored and are reinforced with tangible, positive consequences when they are achieved. This is a mutually rewarding system and gives rise to negotiation and symmetrical movement in older children.

If Bill (age 15), for example, wants to extend his curfew time from 9:00 P.M. to 10:30 P.M. on weeknights, he can negotiate this change by completing the responsibilities designated on the chart. The family therapist can then label his efforts as cooperation and maturity. His parents can grant a privilege rather than give in, and a sensible step in his separation from the family has been accomplished. It is important to remember that having Bill out of the house until 10:30 each night may functionally serve to allow mother and father to spend more time together as husband and wife. If this new arrangement places too many demands for merging on the husband and wife, then Bill's new separating function is placed at risk. Careful monitoring of this situation by the family therapist provides this important information about functions.

Note and Message Centers

As families age and the individuation of their members increases, the message center becomes an important addition to the family's daily life. This simple tool can provide important educational structure. For example, a single working mother of two daughters, ages 16 and 19, wanted help for her older daughter because she wasn't "getting things together." After several family sessions it had become clear that the mother feared her daughters would repeat her history of leaving home without a good education, getting married or pregnant too early, having children, and becoming divorced and thereby left with excessive responsibilities and few resources. The mother's overinvolvement in her older daughter's personal business was pushing her daughter into a position of having to leave home and in fact get out on her own. The daughter, however, did not want to leave home and in fact had planned on living with her mother and sister for at least another year while she worked and prepared herself to go back to school. In her view, she had lived with the consequences of her mother's behaviors and had no intention of repeating those mistakes. Because she was similar to her mother in many ways, however—she was somewhat impulsive, was poorly organized, and tended to procrastinate—the mother became outraged when seeing those behaviors, which reminded her of herself, and lectured her daughter about how poorly prepared and immature she was. In contrast, the mother described the 16-year-old daughter as a "neat kid," who was responsible (cooked meals) and who also told her mother about the older daughter's mistakes.

As this interplay was made clear to the family, the older daughter readily responded to several educational aids, specifically contracts and charts to reflect progress, in order to extricate herself from her position as the irresponsible one. This step alone, however, was not sufficient to restabilize the family interaction patterns because it did not involve enough merging for the mother and daughter. To achieve a form of merging, the message center was instituted, as described in the following transcript example:

> *Therapist:* With the three of you working, going to school, and involved in so many activities, you need to stay connected to each other. After all, what would happen if Mom's car breaks down and she needs to reach one of you to help her out?
>
> *Younger Daughter:* One of us needs to take an automobile repair class. (All laugh.)
>
> *Therapist:* Do you have a place to leave each other messages . . . you know . . . where you are, where you are going, how long you'll be gone, and where you can be reached?
>
> *Mom:* We used to have a bulletin board, the paper is gone and so is the pen. . . . We could put that together.
>
> *Therapist:* Good. You do need something to help you stay in contact with each other. Will you use it? (All agree.)

After a trial week the family came back for a review. The message center had worked well. The mother felt that she had some control, and both daughters discovered they could have more independence while maintaining a feeling of merging; they enjoyed leaving humorous (as well as informative) notes for each other. A month later the system was still working and the family showed great interest in buying an answer-phone. As the mother put it, "It would be fun to hear all our voices and would almost be like having someone home all the time." The daughters were quick to add that their friends could leave messages as well.

Notes from School

It is always important to connect extrafamilial environments, especially the school, with home-based change programs. Asking for notes from school is a simple technique that generates useful feedback and creates congruence across environments. The procedures are simple: a call to the school, an appointment with the appropriate personnel, and an agreement by them to provide parents with daily and weekly feedback about attendance, classroom behavior, and academic performance. With data coming in from school on a regular basis, home programs focusing on responsibilities and privileges can be enhanced.

Relaxation Work

The various approaches to relaxation training (Benson, 1975; Lazarus, 1968) provide payoffs to the family. Not only does relaxation training directly help the individual, but it can be used to legitimize functional relationships. If a separating function is operating, for example, then the family member can escape to privacy in order to relax. If a merging function is operating, then one family member can help another learn the relaxation response.

INTERPERSONAL TASKS

Because communication requires at least two people and because technical aids are rarely used in a vacuum, we include an important third category in education. A necessary and integral feature of functional family therapy is that the therapist assign certain interpersonal tasks designed to produce specific new learning patterns in the family context. These tasks may include practicing at home the communication styles learned in a session, practicing a particular aspect of effective communication in the session itself, rehearsing a difficult situation in one's mind (cognitive rehearsal), and starting a new behavioral style (sometimes by using such artificial props as reminder cards, timers that limit the period of interaction, and token economies). Keeping in mind that assigned tasks must be derived from a functional analysis, family therapists can develop effective tasks by following these guidelines:

1. Design the task to provide an immediate sense of relief or pleasure for each person involved. Although family members may occasionally be asked to do something for the long-term good, in general a task will be effective if each person either enjoys doing it or receives immediate pleasure or relief as soon as it is accomplished.

2. Be sure everyone agrees that the task assigned can be accomplished and will result in mutual payoffs. Even if the therapist believes the family members can accomplish the task, if one or more family members believe it is impossible, they probably will not do it. In general, family members reflect this attitude in a variety of forms (traditionally called resistance). Resistance signals that either the task itself was inappropriate for the identified functions or the functions themselves were inappropriately identified. When therapists encounter resistance, they should return to the therapy phase and develop more effective new labels or more appropriate functions.

3. Have all family members explain the task assignment before they leave the session. (This same procedure is followed in the clarify-style process of therapy.) Therapists must constantly remind themselves that family members and therapists not only may assign dramatically different meanings to the same word or phrase but also may assume different specific behaviors are necessary to carry out specific tasks. To ensure that everyone has common goals, the therapist should make certain that each family member can and will explain the process.

4. Keep the task simple enough to ensure success. Particularly in the early phases of education, even bright family members may have difficulty carrying out behavioral changes that are strong departures from earlier ways of functioning. Keeping tasks simple and providing as many technical props as possible considerably increase the probability of success. Successful completion of tasks allows the family to experience new ways of behaving and to sense that intervention is in fact helpful not just painful. If therapists keep tasks simple and they are not accomplished, the problem probably exists in the functional analysis not in the mechanics of the task itself. In this way, even failures are useful and informative (Palazzoli-Selvini, Boscolo, Cecchin, & Prata, 1978).

5. Make sure everyone is interested in seeing how the others do their part. To the extent that family members see certain tasks as being irrelevant to them personally, the therapist has done an incomplete job of developing a relational picture of the family. If, for example, a mother's attempts to control her anxiety are seen merely as her own thing by her son, the son either does not want to or is not able to see how his behavior, feelings, and thoughts are related to his mother's typical style for dealing with anxiety.

6. Don't force views of reality to change instantly. When families have spent years developing certain attributions, it is unlikely that these can be dramatically changed, even with the most artful new labels. Many adaptive and successful families, in fact, have learned to agree to disagree and to avoid tasks and other forms of interaction that require only one view of reality when, in fact, two or more exist.

7. Develop tasks that allow people to set and attain personal as well as group goals. Too many therapists fall into the trap of developing tasks that help the entire family and forget that altruism becomes difficult if individuals aren't also allowed to pursue their personal goals.

8. Believe in approximation. Do not begin the educational phase with tasks designed to solve the big problem. As numerous authors have stated in one form or another, most families have taken quite a bit of time to develop the maladaptive relationships they bring to the therapist. It is unrealistic to expect that they can produce major changes without having made minor changes first.

9. Keep track of the task. Family members must get the idea that the therapist takes these tasks seriously. Family members can become quite lax in maintaining newly developed interaction styles. If the therapist fails to keep track, the family's "honeymoon" will soon come to an end because behavioral changes will not have been sufficiently well developed to maintain the attitudinal changes that preceded them. When this failure occurs, family members and therapists can become discouraged and even resentful and aggressive toward one another.

10. Create tasks for spectators. Even when a task must be completed by only one person, interdependence and mutual support will be enhanced if spectators also have a formal role, even if it is only a monitoring function. If a task is designed to give a person a sense of autonomy and distance, spectators can

participate by expressly engaging in behaviors that facilitate the distance and autonomy.

Conflict-Management Practice

The conflict-management system illustrated in the excerpt below is most effective in midpointing symmetrical relationships. The system has five steps: (1) An appointment is made to discuss a particular issue: changing the separating function of previous fights to the merging function of problem solving, for example. (2) The single issue is stated clearly, followed by active listening only. (3) Two recent examples are given and are repeated by the partner. (4) The personal impact of the examples is given and is repeated by the partner. (5) Alternatives are discussed, and a temporary solution is agreed to (see Bach & Wyden, 1970).

Therapist: Okay, you both know the procedure for resolving an issue or argument. . . . Who wants to start?

Ted: I have something I'd like to get clear on.

Therapist: Okay, you start. I'll stay out of it. I will keep you on track if you two forget the procedure.

Ted (to Kathy): I have an issue I'd like to discuss. Is this a good time? [Step 1. Alerts Kathy and gets permission. (Note that previously described principles such as source responsibility and directness are also present but will not be designated in this section.)]

Kathy: You have an issue you would like to discuss, and, yes, this is a good time to do it. [Active listening and feedback.]

Ted: My issue is that it is becoming hard for me to ask you what you are doing about certain things that are your responsibility. [Step 2.]

Kathy: Your issue is that you find it difficult to ask me about how I'm handling my responsibilities. [Active listening.]

Ted: Yes. . . . My two most recent examples are waiting too long to balance the checkbook and . . . uh, well . . . not keeping up with the laundry. [Step 3.]

Kathy (to Therapist): Can I say something about that?

Therapist: Not yet. . . . Just repeat back what Ted has said. Let him know you heard him. [Request for active listening and feedback.]

Kathy: Your examples are being late with the checkbook and not keeping up with the laundry. [Active listening.]

Ted: Thanks for listening. Now, the impact that has on me is that I get angry, feel kinda out of control; but I need to know our financial status, and I need clothes for work. I guess I feel I can't tread on your thing, but it's affecting me, and it really grinds on me. [Step 4.]

Kathy: You get angry about this, feel out of control; and you are pissed because it's my thing and the way I do it affects you in some bad ways. Right?

Ted: You got it.

Therapist: We could finish this here, but I want you to solve this one yourselves . . . at home. Use the tape cassette you just bought and have this discussion at home. Record it and bring it back with you next week so we can listen to it together. Remember, stay with the subject at hand, listen to each other, and explore alternatives. Got it? (Both nod agreement.) [Step 5.]

After teaching families the elements of good communication, therapists need to see that these new skills are applied in natural contexts. Cassette tape recorders are often used to enhance at home skills learned in therapy sessions. They are particularly useful in helping families learn effective conflict-management procedures such as fair fighting (Bach & Wyden, 1970).

Family Outings and Projects

Therapists often find it necessary to assign a family outing or project to help the family practice their newfound problem-solving skills. The transfer of lessons from the therapist's office to the home is enhanced by developing new interaction styles under the therapist's guidance and then having the family practice them at home. Without this transition, adaptive styles can become associated too much with the context of the therapist's office, and family members may either come to depend too much on the therapist or reject the therapist's techniques as useless. Both results preclude an efficient and effective termination.

Therapist: One of the reasons problems seem so overwhelming is that they aren't clearly identified and dealt with. This happens because couples hide behind them and keep busy. How can you solve problems if you don't spend any time together? The lack of personal time, as you two well know, is always a problem.

Susan: How do you get time when dogs and kids and jobs are always there gettin' in the way?

Therapist: You make it a priority.

Mark: It's easy if you say it fast.

Therapist: It takes a commitment to a sense of "us-ness" and then it takes practice. [Rationale.] This week I want you two to arrange for 12 hours of personal time. No kids, dogs, phones, or anything else. I want you to check into a motel if necessary. The rules are: No sleeping or leaving and you must talk about personal things . . . each other. You can't talk about the kids or the job. I have here a list of things that all couples need to talk about. It will help you get started. (Hands list to couple with headings such as Trust, Sexuality, Personal Limits, Anger Displays, Romantic Illusions, Centricity—How Important Am I to You, Optimal Distance—When Do I/You Need Space, Personal Boundaries.) [Assigns task.] Do you have any questions?

Susan: That's pretty scary to me.

Mark: I'm ready, sounds sorta interesting.

Susan: Have you ever had any mortalities doing this?

Therapist: Only mortals.

Susan: I know when I'd like to do it . . . Tuesday . . . after I get Sandra off to camp and after my mother leaves, after the dog show. I'd hate to foul that up.

Mark: I gotta work Tuesday. Let's do it this weekend. It should be a priority. Anyway, I can't get off work.

Therapist: You two are getting right into it, that's good. The problem here is that you are both right. You both have legitimate positions. It will be interesting to see how you handle this situation. (Pause.) Before we go any further, I want you both to state your partner's position on this thing. [Requests practice.]

Mark: Susan wants to go Tuesday, so she can get things done . . . get Sandra off to camp, do the dog show, and some other things. I'd like. . . .

Therapist: Before you get into problem solving, let's make sure Susan knows your position. . . .

Susan (interrupting): Mark can't or won't take time off from work Tuesday and wants to do it this weekend.

Therapist: My assignment to the two of you is to resolve this dilemma and spend the 12 hours together discussing the items on the list I gave you. Be clear with one another, try to listen, in fact, repeat back what's being said to you if you get confused. There is a solution somewhere. I'm looking forward to our appointment next week to see what happened.

Mark: Us, too. (Susan nods.)

Therapist: We have some time left so we are going to get into some of the material you brought in regarding the issues you have with one another.

Susan: My main issue is that I want to go to work, but Mark gets furious when I bring the subject up to the point where I just . . . well. . . .

Therapist: That's a big one. If you go to work, do you take time away from your kids or your husband or both? If you don't go to work, do you take time away from yourself? Women for a long time have been told that if the marriage fails or the kids aren't doing well, it's the woman's fault. Men are told to go out, put on the harness, and make money. Sounds like an issue for both of you.

Mark: I just don't think she should work. . . . The kids need her, I need her. . . . It just doesn't seem right. . . . I mean I make enough money.

Therapist: Sounds like there's a pretty heavy price for you to pay if Susan "gets happier." (Uses fingers to place quotation marks.)

Mark: If getting happier means that she leaves me and the kids, then screw it.

Therapist: Tell Susan what your fears are. You know: "The impact of your going to work on me is. . . ." [Requests practice.]

Mark: The impact of your going to work on me is that I'm going to be on my own again, and I don't like that.

Therapist: Susan, share with Mark some of your thoughts about working. You know, how you see it fittin' in, why it's important to you . . . stuff like that. (Holds hands up.) Before you do that, though. . . . Mark, I just want you to listen.

After Susan shares her feelings regarding work, the therapist has Mark repeat back what she has said to him, and the process is reversed, clearing space for alternatives and discussion.

Therapist: Good. Now one additional thing. Mark, by all accounts, you get pretty upset with this subject, and, after the fight, Susan, you withdraw, feel guilty, angry, and confused. When this subject is brought up again, Mark, I want you to just listen to what Susan has to say. Don't react, just listen. Susan, after you have said what's on your mind, just smile and say thanks for listening.

Mark: That's gonna be pretty hard to do.

Therapist: I realize that, but it's important to begin sorting through this information. Here's how you can handle it. When you're by yourself during the next few days, practice what you're gonna do. . . . Imagine the situation and how you are being asked to deal with it now. . . . See yourself in a number of scenes with Susan, and she says "I want to talk about work for a few minutes." See yourself saying "Okay, I'm listening." [Requests cognitive rehearsal.]

Mark: Okay, I'll give it a try.

Therapist (to Susan): Stay with the "I" statements, and don't seek his approval one way or another. This is just information exchange.

Susan: All right.

Therapist: Our time's just about up. Let's make sure we have all of these assignments clear.

Time for Transitions

It is an uncommon family that does not have transition problems. A single parent, fatigued, comes home to hyperactive, sullen, hungry, and attention-starved kids, for example. At this point, two different realities and sets of expectations clash. In another example, a husband works a full day with his career on the line, drives a stressful 45 minutes to his home, and is greeted by his attention-hungry wife (and the minor domestic problems that he has enhanced by his own inattention). He heads directly to the wet bar avoiding everything, hoping that his angry expression will keep his family at a distance.

If these transition periods are not dealt with, they become repositories of conflict and dissatisfaction rather than being the glue that can hold active families together. Family therapists can provide considerable relief to couples and families who feel trapped by these transition periods by assigning a transition task. Once again, the concept is quite simple—allow transitions before making demands and issuing statements—as are the directions— the single parent is allowed 15 to 30 minutes of privacy to take care of his or her business (making baby-sitting arrangements, showering, starting dinner, having a beer); a spouse coming home from work receives similar treatment. Parents of young children can use a timer to let them know when their father or mother is available. After the prescribed time, it is back to normal, and interactions can begin. An underlying assumption of this task is that if the front door becomes a cue for avoidance behavior then problem solving and cooperation are compromised. Transition programs create a positive value for the home and the people in it.

Competence Builders

In family counseling it is often necessary to shore up the re-labeling process with assignments for defining individuals in more desirable ways. These assignments promote acceptance of relabeling as well as of changing roles. For example, a therapist tells a previously "irresponsible, impulse-ridden" 15-year-old boy that if he spontaneously starts an important chore around the house and completes it unsupervised, the therapist will help him use that event when negotiating with his parents for privileges. The therapist and the adolescent then explore what chore the boy could successfully initiate and finish and discover he has two skills that could be utilized. Through a high school continuation program he had learned the basics of automobile mechanics and woodworking. He decides that he will fix the back porch first. He plans and rehearses the project with the therapist to ensure success and completion. In subsequent sessions with the family the completed task can be used as an example of the adolescent's capability and responsibility.

PUTTING EDUCATION IN PERSPECTIVE

Education is not restricted to the techniques listed in this book or in any other book for that matter. Sculpting clay, playing board games, and jogging together are but three of innumerable other activities that can be used to produce lasting changes in family interactions. In other words, there are as many options as there are activities that can be used to facilitate change.

Therapists must remember that techniques are not an end in themselves and are not necessarily to be used forever. They are mediating operations that are often unnecessary or inappropriate once the family has developed stable, adaptive interaction patterns. It is not uncommon for a family in treatment to be simultaneously using a negotiated token system, communication-training exercises for the spouses, reminder cards placed in strategic places like medicine cabinets and lunch boxes, a message center on the refrigerator, graphs on bedroom doors, an appointment calendar indicating the various arranged activities, a commercially produced relaxation cassette audiotape, and a note system with the school. However, very few normal families would be utilizing such educational devices all at the same time, so we expect and hope that families in treatment will eventually interact successfully without all these aids. A change in the use of aids is particularly necessary when families undergo major developmental changes because rigidly adhering to the old techniques could stunt the flexibility and problem solving necessary for families to meet new challenges. During the early periods of therapeutic change, these aids and techniques are invaluable in helping families establish new and productive relationships. In the end, though, it is the process, not the content, that makes the difference between patchup jobs and meaningful change.

SUGGESTED READINGS

Allyon, T., & Azrin, N. H. *The token economy: A motivational system for therapy and rehabilitation.* New York: Appleton-Century-Crofts, 1968. *This classic description of behavior-control procedures details the limits and ranges of token economy systems. Principles of application and their conceptual underpinnings in the behavioral model are well described.*

Bach, G. R., & Wyden, P. *The intimate enemy.* New York: Avon, 1970. *This book is the major statement of conflict-resolution principles and techniques. Though generally applicable to work with couples, these concepts can be applied to all interacting systems either directly or in slightly modified forms.*

Gelfand, D. M., & Hartmann, D. P. *Child behavior analysis therapy.* New York: Pergamon Press, 1975. *This book provides a clear and well-written description of the state of the art of assessment and intervention with children based on social-learning theory.*

Patterson, G. R. *Families: Application of social learning to family life.* Champaign, Ill.: Research Press, 1971. *This book provides a clear description of a range of intervention techniques that can be used with children; the techniques are based on social-learning concepts and empirically sound principles.*

Patterson, G. R., & Gullion, M. E. *Living with children: New methods of parents and teachers* (Rev. ed.). Champaign, Ill.: Research Press, 1971. *This practical handbook of behavior-change techniques and concepts is an excellent adjunct source for intervention in families with young children.*

Stuart, R. B. Behavior contracting within the families of delinquents. *Journal of Behavior Therapy and Experimental Psychiatry,* 1971, 2(1), 1–11. *See comments for Weathers and Liberman (below).*

Stuart, R. B., & Lott, L. A. Behavioral contracting with delinquents: A cautionary note. *Journal of Behavior Therapy and Experimental Psychiatry,* 1972, 3, 161–169. *See comments for Weathers and Liberman (below).*

Weathers, L., & Liberman, R. P. Contingency contracting with families of delinquents and adolescents. In C. M. Franks & G. T. Wilson (Eds.), *Annual review of behavior therapy: Theory and practice* (Vol. 4). New York: Brunner/Mazel, 1976. *This article and those by Stuart and by Stuart and Lott (above) provide comprehensive, clear, and programmatic descriptions of the major techniques of contingency contracting. Pitfalls and critical components of the technique are presented in sufficient detail to allow for replication and evaluation.*

CHAPTER 5

The Family Therapist

Although some have attempted to perform therapy via computers and response panels, it seems that most family therapists will continue to be human–in form if not in function. The new family therapist will find a variety of styles for being a therapist available, styles often too incompletely described to be easily emulated, yet sufficiently embedded in dogma to be at times contradictory. Writings in the behavioral literature as well as the previous chapters in this book generally emphasize the technology of change but rarely tell readers how techniques are applied by the therapist. Statements such as "The parents were persuaded . . ." and "The family realized the importance of good communication" do not indicate how these goals were arrived at. Other articles and books describe therapist behavior by including transcripts of what was said, and some suggest maneuvers such as rearranging chairs and moving people in and out of rooms (Minuchin, 1974; Satir, 1967). While these maneuvers can be beneficial, many therapists who have tried to use them have experienced uneven results. Thinking the problem lies in technology, they either rigidly try to improve the techniques or become disenchanted and try a new set of conceptual and technical approaches. However, the problem often lies not in the technique but in the application. Techniques in themselves are neither good nor bad; their usefulness lies in when, how, and why they are used. Stated differently, surgeons can successfully repair your tissue no matter what their bedside manner. In fact, you can be repaired without ever meeting your surgeon in the social sense. Family therapy, however, requires the therapist to have particular interpersonal qualities.

Family therapists must be reasonably intelligent, though they need not be brilliant. Family therapists must be smart enough to understand the subtleties of many family themes, the complexity of many interactions, and the range of possible communications. However, the importance of intelligence shouldn't be overestimated. The smartest education students don't inevitably make the most sensitive or creative teachers, and the smartest medical school students do not necessarily become the most effective medical practitioners. Thus being reasonably intelligent is a prerequisite, but beyond this minimum level intelligence has relatively little importance.

Of far greater importance is the impact family therapists have: Can we initially create enthusiasm, hope, and specific plans for change? Later, can we help family members move from being merely responsive to us to being able to maintain effective problem-solving styles independently of us? To decide whether a therapist can successfully handle these tasks, two major aspects of the therapist must be taken into account: status characteristics and interpersonal skills.

As we use the term, status characteristics define what therapists are—their sex, age, ethnic and racial identification, and physical attractiveness. Although make-up, grooming, and clothes can modify these characteristics to a minor extent, they are essentially unchangeable. They cannot be appreciably changed through training, shaping, gaining insight, modeling, negotiating, or in any other way. Thus each therapist must learn to appreciate the impact of his or her unique configuration of status characteristics and then learn how to behave in ways that make the impact of these characteristics beneficial. To ignore the impact of these characteristics or to blame clients because they don't respond to them in ways we'd like seriously reduces our therapeutic effectiveness.

Interpersonal skills are the potentially changeable ways in which therapists behave toward clients. Though it may not always be easy, we can learn to smile rather than frown, ask questions rather than give orders, and look attentive rather than look bored. The nature and timing of these and many other specific behaviors powerfully affect the intervention process. Later in this chapter we describe the major characteristics of these behaviors, how they affect intervention, and how we can learn to express them.

STATUS CHARACTERISTICS

Like it or not, when you walk into the room with a family, part of your impact as a therapist depends on what you appear to be. And there are no simple advantages or disadvantages to any given appearance. A young therapist often faces suspicion from the parents ("Do you have teenagers of your own?"), while an older therapist is often perceived by younger family members as being allied with the parents. Similarly, female therapists often face (at best) patronizing behavior from macho male family members, and male therapists may be perceived as insufficiently sensitive. White therapists seeing Black families and Black therapists seeing White families are two more of the many areas where status characteristics play a role.

Knowing these issues do exist can help us identify potential problems in therapy, but how are we to deal with them? Changes in the age, sex, and ethnicity of family therapists are impossible, so we are left with two major options. First, to some extent we can match therapists to families: older married therapists can see older families; Black therapists can see Black families. Such matching has many limitations, however; most family therapists must deal with a wide range of families. Our second option is thus to develop skills to respond to this diversity. Yet how, with respect to status variables, do we develop such skills?

Our clinical and research experience has shown that in the early phases of therapy we must, to a great extent, learn how to meet the expectations of families with respect to status issues. For example, when seeing an obviously traditional (sexist) family, female therapists have much greater positive impact and fewer dropouts if they initially behave in traditional feminine ways: sympathetic, warm, questioning, but not directive. With a liberated family, female therapists can behave assertively and otherwise less traditionally. Similarly, newly trained 25-year-olds often fail miserably if they try to act like experienced therapists, while 55-year-old veterans usually easily have success in directing parents. In other words, every point on each status variable has both potential advantages and disadvantages, but early sessions are generally successful when the therapist appears to behave according to the family's values and stereotypes. If the family sees age as implying wisdom, the older therapist can act as a wise man or woman while the younger therapist probably must rely instead on different skills such as wit, enthusiasm, and sensitivity. If the family views males as strong and females as weak, in early sessions female therapists can avoid being too directive, relying instead on reflective comments and questions.

We realize such statements will rankle many readers, just as they offend our own sensitivities with respect to sexism, racism, and numerous other social problems. However, we also realize that the main goal of therapy is to help families; if families terminate therapy because we blatantly ignore or even oppose their expectations, then we have failed no matter how noble our social ideals. In other words, we feel that our goals in family therapy should be kept separate from our ideals and goals as members of society. A traditional male therapist must be able to help liberated families without forcing his model of the ideal (patriarchal) family on them. Similarly, a radical feminist therapist must not force the wife in a traditional Chicano family to become the equal of her husband and socially independent. We must recognize that families can be adaptive in ways other than ours, and as family therapists we need to learn what these ways are.

Once families have begun to experience change and to develop a sense of trust, then therapists can help them develop alternative concepts and styles of interaction. Traditional wives can learn to accept source responsibility, just as aggressive females can learn to develop positive assertive behavior. Therapists at this point can begin to elicit, prompt, model, and reinforce these alternative interpersonal styles and at the same time help other family members experience them in nonthreatening ways. If, for example, the traditional husband can experience his wife's new assertiveness as greater honesty, which reflects her respect, then he will be likely to attempt to learn new ways to respond adaptively to it. But as long as he perceives her assertiveness as a challenge to his authority, he will resist. (The same goes for therapists!) Thus changes such as these can be demanded of families only after therapists have begun to help them.

In sum, what we are, our status characteristics, influence our therapeutic impact. This impact cannot be ignored, and we should not all try to become the same. In addition, in the early sessions a therapist must learn to behave roughly in ways that correspond to the family's expectations based on the therapist's status characteristics. The therapist can then gain entry and begin to produce change. There is no right way to enter families. A number of vehicles are available, and therapists must learn to utilize the ones that best integrate the unique characteristics of both the family and the therapist. Family therapists should not be other than what they are but instead learn to use what they are to produce change.

INTERPERSONAL SKILLS

Beyond status characteristics, family therapists can vary on two bipolar interpersonal dimensions: relationship behaviors and structuring behaviors (Alexander et al., 1976). These dimensions are independent of one another; therapists can vary from low to high on each of them. In our research, male and female therapists from paraprofessionals to those with doctorates, from relatively inexperienced to quite experienced, from home economists to clinical psychologists, all were either high or low on these two styles. *Relationship* behaviors are those that create an accepting and nonblaming atmosphere with concern for each family member. Included in relationship behaviors are warmth, humor, nonblaming, and integrating feelings and behavior. *Structuring* behaviors are those that control and direct sessions and include directiveness, clarity, specificity, and self-confidence. Appendix A contains specific rating scales for each of these dimensions, so readers can evaluate their own sessions and compare themselves with the following four therapist types.

The Nebish

This therapist, irrespective of age, sex, experience, and dogma, rated low in both relationship and structuring skills. Specifically, this therapist seems unable either to forcefully guide and direct interaction or to relate feelings to behavior. These low raters often fail not by commission but by omission. Not only must the family therapist say the right thing, but he or she must also be able to quickly intercede to prevent family members from saying too much of the wrong thing. The therapist must be active enough to interrupt destructive sequences, to relabel attitudes (hassling becomes concern, obstinacy becomes a search for identity), and to generate enthusiasm and even humor in a family trapped in anger and despair. Therapists low on both structuring and relationship skills are unable to do so and experience repeated dropouts, recidivism, and other discouraging results. They cannot change the family's "game without end" (Watzlawick, Beavin, & Jackson,

1967), and their inability to do so quickly becomes apparent to the family.

Therapists who find that they characteristically are low on both structuring and relationship skills can take a number of approaches to enhance their therapeutic effectiveness. First, many find workshops or courses in assertiveness training to be helpful. Although most assertiveness training courses are not designed specifically for therapists, they can help low raters acquire both the cognitive and the behavioral components of being assertive, particularly in stressful situations. Second, such a therapist can ask the family to go slowly. The therapist can take notes on a clipboard or writing tablet in order to encourage the family to slow down. Family members are amazingly willing to wait for the therapist to write something down if they believe that this information is important and that the therapist needs it either now or later. Third, a therapist can say to the family "Let me think for just a minute," then refer back to notes or simply sit and think of what to say next. Finally, when interactions become overwhelming, the therapist can say "Hold it! Now, starting with you, could you please tell me what you were trying to get across to the rest of the family in the interaction that just occurred?" By asking such a question, the therapist regains control of the interaction without having to be uncomfortably directive or even particularly sensitive to the interpersonal nuances of the interaction.

Sgt. Joe Friday

These therapists are relatively high on structuring skills but low on relationship skills. They are clear, direct, forceful—and cold, distant, and apparently unaware of the feeling aspect of family life. This assessment is not meant to imply that these therapists are truly cold, distant, and unaware. However, they appear that way because they ask many structured questions that emphasize pathology ("How often does he come home late?"), they focus predominantly on behavior to the exclusion of affect ("What did you do then?" instead of "That upset you . . . what did you do then?"), and they act stiff and formal. These therapists, in contrast to the Nebish, do have an impact on families as the structure they impose provides a temporary contrast to family chaos. However, in time they too experience dropouts and failure because most families cannot successfully change their relational atmosphere solely through the use of highly structured programs designed to change behavior. Family therapists with good structuring skills but poor relationship skills often come across to families as having little empathy and as facilitating or at least allowing considerable blaming behavior. The families see these therapists as "too mechanistic, overlooking affective cues given by the family, and possibly . . . either too distant or insincere" (Stanton, 1980b, p. 377). Further, as discussed in the previous chapter, many families are unwilling or unable to respond to a highly structured educational format until their attitudes about relationships have been modified through therapy.

These therapists can benefit from activities designed to enhance their relationship skills. In our clinic, for example, we ask that such therapists pay particular attention to relationships and feelings, even during their everyday social activities. Between classes, while riding elevators, and even in research groups, we ask them (and other trainees with whom they interact) to take extra time to share feelings, ask about others' feelings, and begin reflecting feeling states. They can also benefit from reading literature on interviewing skills (Tyler, 1969) and the traditional client-centered techniques (Rogers, 1951).

The Warm Fuzzy

These therapists, often held in high esteem in traditional schools of therapy, are relatively high in relationship skills but low on structuring. They have few dropouts and are by and large successful, but they take an inordinate amount of time. Families tend to drop out only in later sessions, when the promise of early sessions is not kept. These therapists, through their warmth, humor, and attention to and acceptance of feelings as well as facts, provide a nonblaming atmosphere, create trust, and generate hope in families. However, their inability to be sufficiently clear and directive often results in a failure to capitalize quickly on their therapeutic impact. Although they successfully move the therapeutic focus on relationships and functions, they cannot then create clear and concrete programs to produce rapid change. And, although they model warmth and acceptance, they cannot model good negotiation skills, assertiveness, and source responsibility.

Therapists who find that they can easily develop relationships with family members and facilitate the therapeutic aspects of intervention but cannot make the switch to education can benefit particularly from careful supervision and between-session planning. After each session they can carefully evaluate the therapeutic progress that has been made, then develop (in writing, if possible) specific educational plans for each family member. They can ask themselves "What specific activity can this person engage in to change his or her currently maladaptive behavioral style?" If such therapists have several such plans in mind for each family member when they enter the next session, they find it easy to switch quickly from a therapeutic focus to an educational one. Of course, they must also sometimes struggle with existential issues such as their discomfort in taking direct responsibility for someone else's change and their fear of being rejected by family members. We often find it useful to remind such therapists that in child rearing the truly caring parent not only creates a warm and affective atmosphere but must sometimes also show and tell children what to do, including putting limits on them when their behavior is creating problems for themselves or others.

The Superstar

High on both relationship and structuring skills, these therapists produce rapid change in families and rarely have dropouts. Although of no greater intelligence than other therapists, they are able to quickly create the appropriate therapeutic atmosphere ("joining," in Minuchin's, 1974, terms), then just as quickly introduce control and educational structure to produce change (Stanton, 1980b). They don't begin with contracts, behavior exchanges, and the like, but can, in the context of therapy, quickly develop such techniques. In other words, these therapists first create a situation in which therapeutic techniques will work and decide what needs to be modified. They then develop the appropriate educational techniques to produce those changes.

OTHER ASPECTS OF STYLE

To this point we've implied that anyone—young or old, tall or short, attractive or plain—can produce favorable outcomes in family therapy if he or she develops both high relationship and high structuring skills. On one level this is in fact the case and provides some degree of comfort to those entering the family therapy field. On another level, however, therapists must still develop unique styles that match their own characteristics and the expectations of their clients. A certain behavior of yours, for example, may be interpreted as direct, while the very same behavior in me may come across as overbearing. Similarly, my joke may help relieve tension and change perspective, whereas your joke may appear to reflect insensitivity.

The subtleties of each therapist's impact are beyond simple categorization and cannot be described abstractly in a book. Each of us has a unique blend of physical features and unique patterns of nonverbal cues. In addition, each family has unique expectations. We can never know before the fact exactly what our impact will be or exactly which blend of our various stylistic maneuvers to use. As a result, effective therapists develop (to the extent possible) a range of high structuring skills and a range of high relationship skills. They learn, for example, to structure in one family by asking pointed and specific questions, and to structure in another family by using hand movements to indicate who should talk and who should be quiet. They learn to demonstrate high relationship skills in one family by leaning forward, smiling, and listening attentively. In another family, they ask numerous questions about the members' affective reactions to situations and constantly relabel motives as benevolent.

To give an example, some therapists, both male and female, cannot generate warmth in the traditional sense. They are analytic, thoughtful, and basically undemonstrative. Rather than force themselves to try to become something they are not, we instead urge them to use their analytic abilities, thoughtfulness, and lack of demonstrativeness in ways that create a sense of warmth in the family. Such therapists can ask questions about the affective reactions of family members with the same thoughtfulness and precision that they might use when asking a question during a discussion of research. Even though they may not ask these questions in the traditional warm manner, family members will experience this constant focus on their feelings as reflecting caring and warmth on the part of the therapist.

In sum, there are clearly two major classes of interpersonal skills that successful therapists must possess: structuring and relationship. However, there are no simple formulas as to how these skills may be demonstrated. Thus we can use these skill classes only as guidelines and then utilize supervision and consultation to most effectively develop our unique styles.

SUGGESTED READINGS

Alexander, J. F., Barton, C., Schiavo, R. S., & Parsons, B. V. Behavioral intervention with families of delinquents: Therapist characteristics and outcome. *Journal of Consulting and Clinical Psychology,* 1976, *44*(4), 656–664. *This study was one of the earliest investigations of therapist skill categories in systems and behavioral intervention with families. The article provides specific and operationalized descriptions of both major categories—relationship skills and structuring skills—as well as process and outcome data.*

Rogers, C. R. The necessary and sufficient conditions of therapeutic personality change. *Journal of Consulting Psychology,* 1957, *21*, 95–103. *See comments for Truax and Mitchell (below).*

Rogers, C. R., Gendlin, G. T., Kiesler, D. V., & Truax, C. B. *The therapeutic relationship and its impact: A study of psychotherapy with schizophrenics.* Madison: University of Wisconsin Press, 1967. *See comments for Truax and Mitchell (below).*

Truax, C. B. Therapist empathy, warmth, and genuineness, and patient personality change in group psychotherapy: A comparison between interaction unit measures, time sample measures, patient perception measures. *Journal of Clinical Psychology,* 1966, *22*, 225–229. *See comments for Truax and Mitchell (below).*

Truax, C. B., & Carkhuff, R. R. *Toward effective counseling and psychotherapy.* Chicago: Aldine-Atherton, 1967. *Although based on a humanistic perspective of primarily one-to-one therapy, this classic work emphasizes many therapist qualities and attitudinal sets that transcend this specific intervention modality; of importance are the descriptions of how particular relational impacts are mediated through specific therapist behaviors.*

Truax, C. B., & Mitchell, K. M. Research on certain therapist interpersonal skills in relation to process and outcome. In A. E. Bergin & S. L. Garfield (Eds.), *Handbook of psychotherapy and behavior change* (1st ed.). New York: Wiley, 1971. *Although they do not focus on the family therapy process itself, this article and the works by Rogers, by Rogers, Gendlin, Kiesler, and Truax, and by Truax (above) provide the reader with descriptions of salient dimensions of therapist behavior coupled with careful attempts at operationalization.*

The conceptual underpinnings and research findings may or may not generalize to the family therapy context, but these studies nevertheless provide plausible hypotheses as well as a mandate to carefully evaluate the impact of the therapist.

Tyler, L. E. *The work of the counselor* (3rd ed.). Englewood Cliffs, N.J.: Prentice-Hall, 1969. *This good introductory text describes the therapeutic process from a nondirective point of view. This work contains useful reminders of many potential therapeutic pitfalls.*

PART TWO

ISSUES IN THE APPLICATION OF FUNCTIONAL FAMILY THERAPY

To this point we have reiterated one major philos-ophy: family therapy cannot simply follow a specific set of procedures nor can it utilize only one set of techniques. Instead we have emphasized the importance of the conceptual sets the therapist must hold as well as the therapist's knowledge of basic principles of family functioning and family therapy. Only in this context have we described procedures.

Nevertheless, family therapists must possess some sort of plan to guide them through the various phases of intervention. Our discussion of assessment, therapy, and education provides some sense of temporal progression, but at this point we feel it important to go one step further in order to describe specific goals for each session or group of sessions. Before beginning this description, however, we must first briefly discuss the advantages and disadvantages of entering family therapy with a relatively preplanned progression of events in mind.

The disadvantages all accrue from one major phenomenon: preestablished plans can lead to a loss of therapist flexibility, ingenuity, and spontaneity. Therapists and families alike vary widely on almost innumerable dimensions, so a single plan designed to cover all family contacts is unreasonable. The early experiences of the client-centered movement clearly demonstrate the pitfalls of placing too great an emphasis on what to do, and Carl Rogers himself found it necessary to follow up his major book on techniques (Rogers, 1951) with subsequent writing that emphasized instead the goals and framework of client-centered therapy (Rogers, 1957). Thus while many critics still (inappropriately) fault the client-centered approach for being merely a collection of techniques ("Uh-huh," or "You feel that . . ."), the major thrust of that movement is not so much what the therapist should do as how and why the therapist tries to create certain conditions. In this book we have followed a similar theme, placing at least as much emphasis on the concepts as on the techniques of family therapy.

However, conditions that allow the therapist to be flexible can have a heavy price: confusion and uncertainty. Insufficient structure can produce for the therapist a sense of aimless wandering, lack of control, hopelessness, and sometimes anger toward the family. If families are allowed to control the session, then their pathology is most likely to emerge. One can argue that such a process can be helpful diagnostically, but if the family pathology includes destructive interactions, resistance to change, and dropping out of therapy, then we can ill afford much of its occurrence. To take a cynical (yet realistic) stance, even under the best circumstances family pathology can be a powerful antagonist to change. When therapists do not provide an effective therapeutic structure, then change becomes more than difficult; it becomes improbable if not impossible. Thus despite the risk of loss of flexibility, family therapists must enter the therapeutic arena with a relatively clear, preestablished agenda. In Chapter 6 we describe the sequence of goals that constitute this agenda and how they are met in each of the major phases of intervention.

In Chapter 7 we describe the different developmental stages of families, some of the various family structures, and several characteristic themes encountered in troubled families. Understanding these developmental phases, the various family structures, and family themes enables the therapist to efficiently select the specific goals and change techniques appropriate for each family. Although effective family intervention involves numerous common elements, the unique aspects of each family require that these common elements be used in different ways. Conceptual, technical, and interpersonal skills are prerequisites for working with all families, as are such particular techniques as relabeling, nonblaming, establishing a relationship focus, and providing communication training. All families must be assessed, their attributional and motivational sets modified, and their particular behaviors changed through various educational procedures. However, family therapists see families that differ from one another in many specific ways and that require different techniques and emphases at different times. To cite but one example, a therapist cannot focus on the marriage relationship in a single-parent family, whereas in two-parent families this focus is possible. It is thus necessary for therapists to appreciate how families and individual members differ from one another and to recognize how different therapeutic maneuvers must be applied in different families.

Family developmental phases have a tremendous effect on the specific behaviors of family members, on their expectations and goals, and on the types of interventions that can be effective with them. In addition, these phases often involve changes in particular family structures and processes that generate particular problems and require particular interventions (Stanton, 1980b). All families are, at different times, in one or more of three major phases: integration and reintegration (fitting together), maintenance, and exiting (letting go). Family therapists need to understand how these phases determine what a family can do. Parents of a young infant, for example, cannot allow their child as much freedom as can parents of a teenager. Therapists must also be familiar with the changing demands on family members as they move from one phase to another and with how family members can become confused when the rules that operate successfully in one phase are no longer appropriate or adaptive in another.

CHAPTER 6

The Anatomy of Family Therapy

Each major phase of intervention in families has unique goals and therapeutic procedures, which are described in this chapter. These phases are: (1) entering the family: session one, (2) planning between sessions one and two, (3) session two, (4) the middle stage of intervention: education, (5) the latter stage of intervention: unfinished individual and dyadic business, and (6) termination: making the therapist obsolete. The reader will note that in this chapter we restate principles and techniques described earlier. We think it important to run the risk of redundancy, however, in order to provide a sense of the flow of intervention.

ENTERING THE FAMILY: SESSION ONE

As described earlier, this session is a blend of both assessment and therapy. Families begin their contact with therapists by presenting different blends of behavior, affect, attributions, and cognitions. In encountering these opening moves, therapists attempt to send two powerful messages: "I can help you get things under control" and "I am a caring person." The therapist must remember that by themselves family members have been unable to resolve the problems they face, and they need the therapeutic structure to begin to change in a positive direction. As a caring person, the therapist transmits the message that he or she is interested, involved, and committed to understanding the family and helping it change. Family members who feel abused, neglected, or misunderstood must believe that they will be heard. Family members who feel out of control must believe that the therapist is capable of helping them develop a sense of control and order and is willing to do so. In order to transmit these messages to the family, the therapist routinely follows certain procedures in response to the family's presentation of behavior, feelings, cognitions, and attributions.

Clarifying the Meaning of
Each Family Member's Behavior and Descriptions

Family members possess idiosyncratic and unknown (to the therapist) meanings for the phenomena they describe or present. A statement by one family member about another such as "He doesn't care" can mean one of many things, including "He is characteristically withdrawn," "He doesn't use words that I interpret as caring," "When I become hysterical he leaves," "He behaves in a caring way but I distrust his motives." In the first session the therapist must identify the idiosyncratic meaning of each member's behavior and descriptions to avoid ascribing an inappropriate meaning. Although members of maladaptive families are used to being misunderstood, it does the therapist little good to become yet another inappropriate or misleading component of the system. To emphasize this point, let us return to Carol's family, which was discussed in Chapter 2.

> *Therapist* (entering room with family): Please be seated. (Looks at Mother.) Does everyone know you called me because Dr. Jones suggested I might help?
> *Mother:* Yes . . . uh . . . Carol's problem is . . . ah . . . he thinks maybe it's psychological. There doesn't seem to be any physical reason for it.
> *Therapist* (looking at Father): What seems to be the problem?
> *Mother:* Her stomach aches. . . . She is home from school two or three times a week now. I never know when the nurse is going to call.
> *Therapist:* What happens when she does?
> *Mother:* The nurse? Well . . . I . . . sometimes she wasn't able to get me 'cause I was at school, so Tom had to get her. Now I mostly stay home. I dropped two classes. Or else I give them my friend's number, and I call her when I'm at school.

Therapist: Uh-huh. (Looks at Father, then at Carol, then at Father.)

Father: I just couldn't keep being interrupted. This computer thing at work is a mess.

Therapist: So you aren't able to help out very much?

Father: No . . . I just. . . .

Therapist (interrupts, looks at Mother): And you end up having to drop classes. Have you always been the one responsible for Carol?

Mother: Well, I am . . . I am the mother in this family.

Unless the therapist is careful here, he or she could make inappropriate assumptions about the mother's meaning. Being "the mother in this family" could mean she feels trapped in a role, or it could mean she feels she has a highly valued role, to cite two of many alternatives. Without clarification, the therapist could draw some highly inappropriate conclusions. In this family, the therapist clarified meaning while continuing a relational focus.

Therapist: Carol, what does that mean when your mom says that she is the mother in this family?

Carol (shrugging): I don't know . . . that she had me?

Therapist (to Carol): Had you? You mean gave birth to you?

Carol: Yeah.

Therapist (to Mother): Is that what it means?

Mother: Well, yeah, but . . . no, it's just that, when she hurts, I hurt too. Maybe I am just too sensitive.

This last remark opens new avenues and lets the therapist know that at this point the mother's messages center primarily on her affective (and perhaps symbiotic) relationship with her daughter. She in fact may feel trapped or she may feel highly valued, but for now her statement has a particular affective configuration. Pursuing all family relationships in the context of this affective configuration would appear to be a promising direction. Without the clarification process that led to knowledge about the affective configuration, however, the therapist might have pursued a different and most likely less productive direction.

Establishing an Interdependent Relationship among Family Members

Although family members are usually quite aware of the misery others produce for them, they are often unaware of the interdependence of the family's behaviors and feelings. The traditional mother-in-the-middle, for example, knows that she is frustrated, trapped, and desperate. She also knows her position entitles her to know secrets, such as her daughter's sexual conflicts (about which the father cannot be told) and the father's sense of confusion in dealing with the daughter. What the mother fails to see, however, is how her position also creates and maintains unwanted sequences. By threatening, for example, to tell her daughter's secrets to the father, the mother produces the very chain of avoidance behaviors in her daughter that she complains about. Similarly, by being more reasonable than the father, she fosters his feelings of confusion and the "unreasonable" outbursts that she feels force her into a moderating role. This interdependence of behavior, thoughts, and feelings must be constantly highlighted by the therapist.

Relabeling and Nonblaming to
Create an Atmosphere Conducive to Change

The procedures of clarification and establishment of a relational focus must be performed in a relabeling and nonblaming context. The family must be helped to see each member as a victim. One important clue to the therapist that new labels are in order is the occurrence of redundancies in the opening stories told by the family members. As descriptions of sequences, feelings, cognitions, and attributes are repeated, the therapist through relabeling begins to challenge the family's reality, creating a new one that describes each family member in different and nonblaming terms. Consider the following excerpts from Paul's family, who began a session describing how Mom responded to Paul's "getting lippy" by hitting him first with a belt, then switching to a broken broom handle when Paul kicked her.

> *Mother:* . . . I think I'd have just beat him to death if he hadn't kept screaming.
> *Therapist:* Father, where were you during all of this? [This unexpected question was designed to move the focus off the mother/child dyad and to refocus on the entire network of family relationships.]
> *Father:* Upstairs, hangin' sheet rock.
> *Therapist:* So, let's see . . . Father, you were upstairs hanging sheet rock; Mom, you were in the kitchen doin' something; and, Paul, you were cruisin' around wondering "What do I get to do. . . . If I bug somebody somethin' will happen."

In providing this summary the therapist simultaneously (1) described a family sequence that included everyone in the relational focus; (2) began to relabel Paul as "bored," not just "lippy"; and (3) blamed no one.

And later in the same family:

Mother: I just can't help myself. . . . Once I get started I just. . . .

Therapist (interrupting): Just hang in there. That has to happen in families. [Nonblaming.] And it is a contact [a new label for the relational outcome of the beating sequence], but not the most pleasant form of contact. [A nonblaming stance to describe a quite violent interchange.]

Assigning Homework to Make Change Tangible

In this last part of the initial session, the therapist and family develop the therapeutic contact. We think of it as "slamming the door" so that the family has a difficult time returning to their pretherapy manner of interacting. One major component of the homework assignment is the designation of the next therapeutic contact. With most families, it is unrealistic and inappropriate to simply schedule a session for the "same time next week." When they arrive for the first session most families either are in a state of crisis or have settled down to a relatively stable situation of unhappiness and inefficiency. In either case it is unwise to allow the family to experience an entire week of interaction after only one therapeutic contact. Thus most second sessions are planned for two or three days after the first session. Because this contact occurs so soon, the therapist can suggest relatively minimal homework activities for the next day or so, yet still give the family the clear message that the therapist operates with plans and procedures.

Because the therapist may not understand the family sufficiently to create a legitimate task assignment, most initial assignments simply extend an issue discussed in the first session. For example, a parent and child who report strong disagreement and considerable arguing on a particular issue may be asked to list their feelings about the issue on paper. Then they are instructed to exchange these papers without discussion so that each can understand the other's viewpoint without having to experience the tension of an argument. Or a husband who complains that his wife doesn't pay enough attention to him may be asked to write down a list of suggested activities for them to do together, one of which the wife may choose to pursue. Because the time between sessions is short, it may not even be necessary for the wife to pursue the activity; having the couple begin to deal with the issue under the therapist's guidance will be sufficient to continue the change process.

Finally, family members should be made aware of the fact that failing in their assignment is not a major problem. At this stage of therapy, failure simply means that the family is frightened and discouraged or that the therapist has had little time to understand what each member wants and needs. The initial homework assignment is not designed to cure everyone; it is designed so that family members can begin to experience a different way of relating to each other.

PLANNING BETWEEN SESSIONS ONE AND TWO

Contrary to popular opinion, much of the important therapeutic work is accomplished by the therapist not during sessions but between them, particularly between the first two sessions. During this time therapists can sit back, removed from the intensity of the first session, and sort things out. We have developed a list for therapists to use as a guide. In using this list, therapists write down the extent to which they met certain goals for each family member during the first session. The goals are: clarifying meaning, relabeling and nonblaming, establishing a focus on relationships, and assessing interpersonal impacts (functions).

By checking themselves on these major goals, therapists can begin to make sense of the family network. "Did I clarify each person's meaning enough to understand his or her interpretations of reality? Did I relabel and nonblame each person so they can *all* begin to see themselves and the others as victims not malevolent causes? Did I integrate each family member's feelings, thoughts, and behaviors into a relationship focus, so they can begin to see their interdependence?" If the answer to any of these questions for any family member is no, the therapist realizes that the highest priority in the next session must be to answer these questions in the affirmative. Then, the therapist can move to the somewhat less technical (but just as crucial) step of identifying the relational impact of each person's behavior and the sequences in which they interact. As described earlier, the relational impact is the function—the reason that families maintain apparently senseless and painful interaction patterns. Therapists differ in how readily they can identify these functions, and functions are not often apparent in the first session (although meeting the goals described above will help to bring them forth). Nevertheless, therapists cannot simply sit back and wait for functions to become apparent. Instead, based on the admittedly sketchy information derived from the first session, they must create an at least plausible explanation of how and why this family operates the way it does. The Family Assessment Worksheet in Appendix B is designed to help therapists arrive at this explanation.

A replica of a completed list of goals exemplifies this process. (The reader, without having seen this particular family, may find some of the therapist's comments nonsensical. However, we think readers will find it more useful to see a real list than to see one that is more understandable but not as representative.) In this family Father had recently retired after over 20 years in the Navy, during which time he had been at sea for long periods of time. The older son, Ray (17 years old), had been arrested for a burglary that had been committed while he was awaiting sentence for two prior burglaries. The younger son, Bob (14 years old), was not mentioned in the referral as a problem but appeared high on drugs when the session began. Father was small, somewhat disheveled looking, and generally passive. He was cognitively and behaviorally rigid. Mother was large, outgoing, and appeared to be self-assured. Ray was tall, handsome, and initially seemed arrogant. Relabeling and active listening by the therapist, however, produced by the end of the session numerous cues from Ray of affiliation and dependence.

In the clarify-meaning panel (Table 6-1) the therapist recollects a fairly successful session; the notes indicate that he felt meanings had been reasonably clarified for three of the family

TABLE 6.1. Clarify meaning

Mother	Cynical but "straight." Sounds more hostile than she is. Much brighter than she appears to be.
Father	Shows feelings but won't discuss until asked. Uncomfortable with nuance and innuendo. Cognitively concrete and rigid.
Older Son	Argumentative as hell but will respond if stuck with. Seems to like being talked and listened to.
Younger Son	Fuzzy. He confused me so I laid off him. Stick with him!

members. His comments are personal reactions and reminders of stylistic aspects that initially threw him off. With Bob, he recognizes his own confusion and further realizes that he ignored Bob (failed to clarify his meaning) because Bob confused him. This realization will be helpful in two ways: first, as a technical issue, it reminds him to pursue Bob and, second, as a conceptual issue, it provides a possible clue to the interpersonal impact of Bob's behavior (if you confuse people—even therapists!—they leave you alone).

In the relabel-nonblame panel (Table 6-2) the therapist feels Father and the two sons were successfully relabeled and nonblamed—that is, the therapist was able to cast their behavior and

TABLE 6-2. Relabel and nonblame

Mother	I tried twice but she pulled a "Yes, but" on me. Why?
Father	Return home from service—stranger—intruder. Can't help but feel a bit like an outsider.
Older Son	Bears brunt of confusion over Father's return.
Younger Son	Holding back to protect self.

feelings in a different light, a light in which they could be seen as victims of circumstances not as malevolent. Regarding Mother, the therapist is uncertain. He remembers two major attempts at new labels, both of which he feels were rejected by Mother. This realization gives rise to many questions but also helps the therapist develop a focus. Why won't she let herself be relabeled as a victim? Is it a therapeutic issue—won't she allow the therapist to control her? Or is she setting herself up as the bad guy so she will be rejected? Or were the new labels so outlandish she simply couldn't accept them (even if they did put her in a more benign light)? In such a situation a therapist cannot always enter the second session with absolute certainty about which hypothesis is correct, but having the questions listed along with the most likely answer can help the therapist focus immediately on relevant aspects of family relationships.

The ability of the therapist to adopt a relationship focus was, in his eyes, mixed (Table 6-3). In general, he felt he did a good job of tying Mother, Father, and Ray together in an interdependent way. Notice, however, that he is concerned about the fact that Father seemed to reject this interdependent view because he

TABLE 6-3. Establish a focus on relationships

Mother	Yes. I constantly tied her behavior to Father's presence/absence. She is the "hub."
Father	? I tried to tie him in, but he kept on with his "absolute" right and wrong statements. Does he see himself as isolated?
Older Son	Yes. I reinterpreted all his "screwing up" as being a function of parental uncertainty.
Younger Son	No. My relational statements were all about Mother/Father/Older Son.

kept responding with absolutes ("Well, even if a father is away in the military, his son should still obey his mother's authority"). Bob, in contrast, was not consistently seen in relational terms, which is reflected both in this panel and in the clarify-meaning panel. To the therapist, this omission signals a necessary focus for the next session to avoid the possibility that Bob will be seen as a family isolate—a member whose maladaptive behavior is not a component of the entire system's functioning.

In the interpersonal-impact panel (Table 6-4) the therapist tries to develop a picture for himself of the possible payoff each

TABLE 6-4. Determine interpersonal impact (function)

Mother	Maintains central role as "boss" but protects Father by verbally agreeing with all his (irrelevant) rules—merging.
Father	Distance and irresponsibility! By running the home on rules, he never has to take personal responsibility.
Older Son	Distance-autonomy. To identify with Father would mean being impotent. Elicits more respect from Mother than she gives to Father. Yet because she argues more with him than with Father this serves to also protect Father. (No wonder Father appears not to be interested in change!)
Younger Son	Is "loved" more because he is withdrawn? Withdrawal elicits contact?

family member receives from the apparently unpleasant state of affairs. He is, of course, not equally certain about all his hypotheses, but the picture he has created does, at least, provide a plausible and comprehensive model that he can take into the next session.

SESSION TWO

The goals for Session Two derive from the conceptual work accomplished between Sessions One and Two. As a first item the therapist attempts to complete the list of goals developed after Session One. In the process, however, the therapist also begins to verify (or reformulate) hypotheses about interpersonal impact by asking questions and observing behavior. With the family in the example above, the therapist might, for instance, first talk to Bob and then ask each of the other family members to describe interactions with Bob on the previous day. Is it the case that when he is quietly doing his own thing people seek him out? Does Father seem to be more affectionate toward him because he doesn't overtly reject Father's rules (as Ray does)?

In clarifying these for himself the therapist also continues to help the family members see themselves in a different light. Father, for example, begins to see Ray not just as an "obstinate snot" but as the older son trying to grow up but not knowing how to in any way other than being oppositional. The family can also begin to see that, although Father's return was eagerly anticipated by all, it involved a confusing new authority pattern for the sons, who weren't sure how much Mother was still in charge. Finally, they can begin to see how the children were afraid to wholeheartedly follow Father's rules because they weren't sure whether Mother would interpret their doing so as moving away from her.

In helping the family members see themselves in a different light the therapist did not verbalize all his hypotheses. Protecting Father, for example, may be a true function but nevertheless an insulting (or defensiveness-arousing) concept to Father. Thus the concepts are couched in gentle (or positive or acceptable) ways. In this sense a therapist is not always truthful and open because such openness may be interpreted by the family as blaming. Instead, the therapist constantly asks "How can I come up with a plausible *and* nonblaming *and* interactional reformulation that will help each family member to want to change, to experience hope, and to see the other family members also as victims and participants?"

In addition to putting a heavy emphasis on therapeutic techniques during this second session, the therapist begins to move as quickly as possible to the educational phase of intervention. In difficult families requiring an extended therapy phase, education continues to consist of relatively simple homework assignments and communication training, while the affective, perceptual, and conceptual realms continue to be the major focus of intervention.

THE MIDDLE STAGE OF INTERVENTION: EDUCATION

The education, or skill-building, phase of intervention, may take weeks or months. Building on successful therapeutic changes, the therapist targets specific maladaptive interactional sequences, skill deficits, areas of ignorance, and maladaptive emotional reactions. As described in Chapter 4, the therapist uses three kinds of educational tools--communication training, technical aids, and interpersonal task assignments—to produce a range of specific changes in the targeted areas. In the case above, for example, Mother and Father learn effective communication behaviors, then begin to model them for the children (this technique has both the direct effect of improving communication and the indirect effect of reducing the children's confusion because they can see the parents make clear decisions); Father learns to effectively monitor Bob's schoolwork and provide feedback; Ray enrolls in and attends a technical training program in return for personal freedom at night and use of the car; Mother takes a community college course and learns assertiveness skills.

THE LATTER STAGE OF INTERVENTION: UNFINISHED INDIVIDUAL AND DYADIC BUSINESS

Throughout the educational phase of intervention, the functional family therapist has been constantly emphasizing "family-ness"—the interdependent nature of behaviors, feelings, and thoughts. All family members have been involved in successfully completing tasks that enhance family functioning, and all have been trained to communicate in effective and adaptive ways. However, to be adaptive, all systems must also have well-defined and well-functioning subsystems. Young children must be helped to begin the process of individuation. Adolescents must begin the process of exiting and developing extrafamilial relationships. Spouses must be helped to develop both the marital relationship and relationships outside the family that will meet economic, emotional, and other individual and interpersonal needs. Thus during the latter stage of intervention, therapists begin to help individuals and dyads separate from one another in adaptive and mutually beneficial ways. To cite an example, a mother and father may be helped to stop using the children to mediate their husband/wife issues. In another family, parenting, decision-making, and general communication processes may be working efficiently, and the family may be quite capable of resolving conflicts and crises as they emerge; but the parents may desire additional changes in the marital relationship independent of family and parenting issues. In this instance, the marriage partners may be seen as a dyad with the rest of the family on hold for a while.

Also during this stage of intervention individuals may begin to make certain lifestyle changes. With a well-functioning family, the man or woman experiencing a midlife crisis may now have the freedom and permission to engage in alternative vocational and educational programs. Teenagers may make the transition from traditional academic pursuits to vocationally oriented technical training. Grandparents may develop new marital and extrafamilial relationships and pursuits so they need not be tied too tightly to the family.

Helping parents develop new marital and individual relationships apart from the children produces positive effects for both the parents and children. As they begin to engage in their own exiting process or plan to complete it, the children can see that the marital relationship is no longer so dependent on them. They can then maintain family ties out of choice not coercion and can also experience integration in their new extrafamilial relationships.

TERMINATION: MAKING THE THERAPIST OBSOLETE

With families dropping out of therapy so frequently, termination in a positive sense is often sadly infrequent. However, Parsons and Alexander (1973), using the functional family model with a population of delinquent families (a difficult population to be sure), cut the dropout rate to 17%, a vast improvement. Thus termination is a realistic goal and one that can be generally attained in this model. But how does a therapist know that the time for termination is near? In general the therapist uses three criteria: cessation of problems, the development of efficient family processes, and the existence of mutual payoffs.

Cessation of Problems

There are both subjective estimates ("Yes, we're much happier") and objective estimates (observed increases in adaptive behaviors) that problems have ceased. The father no longer berates, the mother no longer becomes hysterical, and the son no longer comes home stoned. As families experience this cessation of problems, in one form or another they give the therapist the message "We can do it ourselves or at least try." Therapists can facilitate this process by agreeing with the family and giving them the clear message that if things don't work they are always welcome to return.

Efficient Family Processes

Data from numerous family-interaction research studies demonstrate that adaptive families can be distinguished from maladaptive families on a number of content-free stylistic measures such as equality of talk time (adaptive families have more equal input), participation in conflict resolution situations (all contribute rather than becoming sullen and withdrawn), humor, and source responsibility (family members acknowledge direct responsibility and do not blame abstract forces such as God or "all the other kids") (Parsons & Alexander, 1973). After seeing improvement in these processes, the therapist can be optimistic that the family is capable of maintaining adaptive functioning. However, if families report that problems have ceased but that the family interaction style continues to be maladaptive, the therapist can expect a rerun in the near future. Thus therapists must be sensitive to the degree to which the family spontaneously adopts new problem-solving and communication styles. With families that allow the therapist to continue to generate creative solutions (through task assignments, for example) and fail to spontaneously adopt new adaptive interaction styles, the therapist must place special emphasis on developing approximations of adaptive interaction patterns. In other families, once the members experience the beneficial impact of changing their interactional processes in one area, they can generalize to all new problem areas without additional help from the therapist. In such circumstances, termination can occur quickly.

Mutual Payoffs

Finally, the therapist must be able to see from each family member's perspective how the new family style grants enduring payoffs to all. If a father has been drawn into the style through guilt, for example, he may contribute for a while to problem cessation and a more adaptive family process. If, however, his increased involvement does not involve a functional payoff for him, then he will tend to reduce his contributions as time goes on. Furthermore, therapists must be careful not to assume that a mere reduction in problems will be a sufficient payoff for each family member. Many cases have clearly shown that, although family members are happy to see the removal of symptoms, this payoff is not sufficient to ensure that the new adaptive interaction style will be maintained (Johnson & Christensen, 1975; Wahler, Leske, and Rogers, 1979).

SUGGESTED READINGS

Haley, J. *Problem-solving therapy.* San Francisco: Jossey-Bass, 1976. *The major strength of this basic work is its clear and straightforward description of family change techniques. Although the book is rich in theory, the straightforward and practical style allows for easy translation into specific interventions.*

Minuchin, S. *Families and family therapy.* Cambridge, Mass.: Harvard University Press, 1974. *The written descriptions and visual schematics in this book provide an excellent model for conceptualizing family process and structure. Clear case illustrations and descriptions of techniques give readers numerous vehicles for creating family change.*

Stanton, M. D. Family therapy: Systems approaches. In G. P. Sholevar, R. M. Benson, & B. J. Blinder (Eds.), *Handbook of emotional disorders in children and adolescents: Medical and psychological approaches to treatment.* New York: Spectrum, 1980. *See comment for Stanton, "Strategic approaches to family therapy" (below).*

Stanton, M. D. Strategic approaches to family therapy. In A. S. Gurman & D. P. Kniskern (Eds.), *Handbook of family therapy.* New York: Brunner/Mazel, 1980. *This article and Stanton, "Family therapy" (above), are excellent reviews of the basic principles of systems-therapy approaches and of populations treated with these approaches. Techniques and concepts are clearly described and contrasted.*

CHAPTER 7

Special Family Phases, Structures, and Themes

The family developmental phases of integration, maintenance, and exiting require variations in the applications of therapeutic concepts and techniques. These phases change as a result of both time and circumstance. Time produces changes in family phases because members leave and enter the family through such processes as birth and maturing. Circumstances produce changes in family phases through such processes as divorce, illness, remarriage, death, and job demands that require periods of time away from the home. Families differ in the ways they encounter and adapt to the changes brought on by time and circumstances, and these differences manifest themselves in particular family structures and particular family themes. In order to prepare the family therapist for these differences, this chapter describes each of the family developmental phases and highlights some of the characteristic family structures and themes that are found in each.

FAMILY BEGINNINGS:
THE PHASES OF INTEGRATION AND REINTEGRATION

Integration is characteristic of systems in which new relationships are being created. In new marriages, for example, the two individuals who come together have unique and sometimes potentially incompatible histories, biological characteristics, needs, illusions, and stereotypes. Making decisions on how to share resources, lifestyles, and an indefinite future requires a process of fitting together. As individuals become intimate and share responsibilities, they must develop a wide range of mutually agreed-on rules for interaction; these rules cover both the content and the process of their relationship. *Content rules* concern the facts of the relationship, including such issues as what kind of car to buy, how frequently to have sex, how clean is a clean house, and what to have for dinner. Content issues, though often difficult to resolve, are nevertheless usually easier to understand and negotiate than *process rules,* which concern the procedures of relationships: who initiates intimacy and in what ways, how can each partner get away for a while without signaling rejection, and how do partners resolve conflicts. Although content rules such as car preferences and even the frequency of sex are generally transitory, the process rules developed during integration remain quite fixed and resistant to change. For example, if a husband who has traditionally been the one to initiate sex stops doing so after 15 years of marriage, such a change is likely to create considerable stress. Even if the wife doesn't necessarily enjoy his sexual advances, his failure to continue initiating often engenders depression, affairs, or related phenomena that signal her reaction to this relationship redefinition. To restate Haley's (1963) point, the couple may think that they are struggling over sex as a content issue, but in fact they are struggling with the process issue of who initiates sex and what this process means to them.

The integration phase offers great potential for prevention. Prevention is relatively easy during this phase because family members are not locked into a particular style or styles. If, for example, a spouse or a spouse-to-be changes to direct negotiating rather than giving in and whining during the early stages of relationship formation, probably little chaos will ensue. The same change after 12 years, however, can well produce a totally frightened, confused, and resistant mate. People tend not to work hard on changing patterns during the integration phase of their relationships, however, they see this phase as a transitory period and thus ignore destructive themes and rituals that are developing. Newlyweds assume that the other will change for the better in time. Or new parents assume that the child will grow out of it, so they give in and let the child sleep with them. Those who work in clinics for children often see the results of letting such a situation become stable: bed wetting, sleep walking, nightmares, and cessation of the parental sexual relationship (sometimes a function not unwelcomed by one of the spouses).

One major complication in the integration process of newlyweds (or new intimates of a less traditional form) can be the spouses' families of origin. If new partners have failed to complete the exiting process from their families (see discussion of this process later in this chapter), they can find themselves in relationship configurations that seriously jeopardize the process of integration. When these configurations develop, the family therapist must often include the families of origin in treatment.

A different kind of integration problem involving the spouses' parents occurs when aging parents move in with their offspring. This integration into the home is often disruptive, confusing, and unmanageable. Previously established roles are threatened, parent/child transactions are cross-circuited, and husband/wife conflict and intimacy may take new forms. For example, consider the case of a grandmother who comes to live with her daughter, her daughter's husband, and their three children (ages 6, 9, and 14). A transcript from an initial session with husband and wife identifies and highlights the issues.

> *Therapist:* What brings you to see me?
>
> *Mother:* Well, my mother recently moved in with us, and things went pretty well, uh, well . . . at first, but I'm starting to have some real trouble with the whole thing. Ever since my dad passed away, I. . . .
>
> *Therapist* (interrupting): Before we get into that I'd like to get more information. (Turns to husband): When your wife says that she is starting to have some trouble with this situation, what does she mean?
>
> *Father:* Well, Peg, Sharon's mother, means well, but she sort of gets too involved, especially with the kids. It's been hard on all of us. We're more crowded, and there's less privacy, and plus she likes the house hotter, and we have to cook special food . . . a whole bunch of things.
>
> *Therapist:* It sounds like you two are doing a lot to take care of her. What does . . . uh, er, Peg do to take care of you two? [Relational emphasis and relabeling.]
>
> *Mother:* Uh, what do you mean . . . take care of us?
>
> *Therapist:* I realize that it may be hard to think of it in these terms, but she is your mother, and she probably still wants

to do good things by you. Not to let her do anything would probably make her feel sort of left out, like a fifth wheel. How have you included her in the family?

Mother: Well, she does help out with the kids, especially our youngest one, but it's the kind of help I can do without.

Therapist: You mean she's not a good parent?

Mother: Well, no, but some of the things she does just drive me up the wall.

Father: Peg speaks her mind, and Sharon doesn't always agree, especially when it comes to how we have raised our kids. But they are good kids basically. It's just since Peg moved in that we have had some discipline problems.

Therapist: Can you be more specific?

Father: Well, rather than fight with Peg, Sharon doesn't interfere when Grandma and the kids are doing something, even when the kids do something they know they shouldn't do.

Therapist (to Sharon): Oh, you lose power as a mother in the presence of your own mother. Have the kids picked up on this?

Mother: I hadn't thought quite that way, but . . . ya, sure, the kids seem to know they can get away with more.

Therapist: Well, that's understandable. She wants to help out. You could probably use some help with the kids, but she has to understand that you and Frank here are the heads of the household. If she doesn't understand or follow the rules, as they are, you two could have your hands full. Will Peg come in with you during our next session? [Recasting the problem as the result of inefficiency rather than as the result of one person's badness.]

Mother: Yes, I'm sure she would love to meet you. And maybe we could work something out.

Therapist: Good! Now, then, what are some of the other problems facing the two of you?

During the rest of the initial session the therapist unravels similar themes of help and hindrance, while also exploring Mother's feelings of being a daughter in her own house and Father's feeling that he has to be more rational, better dressed (no bathrobe and sweat socks), and more in control of things. From a functional viewpoint, Grandma's inclusion into the family had diffused her daughter's role as a parent while redefining the marital relationship because of Father's new role as more the man of the house. His sudden shift from passive overseer to active meddler was uncomfortable for both partners. To further complicate matters, the loss of privacy made conflict resolution difficult (the couple found themselves fighting late at night and on the way to parties). In addition the combination of lenient Grandma and now strict Father had substantially upset parenting processes, with all children beginning to act out the change in structure.

The solution to this situation was quite simple. After the therapist met with both parents and Grandma in order to extensively relabel and establish common expectations and aspirations, the parents were able to settle back into their previously accepted roles. Grandma became a helpful third adult and established her role as a welcome guest and special person by allowing her daughter to show her how she did certain things and what strategies she was currently using with the children. A subsequent family meeting solidified the changes. An open discussion, led by Mother, concerned Grandma's role in the family and how everyone could help her feel welcome by not placing unnecessary demands on her. Any special requests were to go to Mother and Father, just as they had in the past. This procedure, as Mother explained, would allow Grandma to teach the kids her special recipes and to play card games (of which Grandma knew many). Father was to back off, Mother was again the central parent figure, Grandma felt accepted and needed, and the children were able to enjoy her company.

Other events such as retirement, the adoption of a child, or the inclusion in the family of a foreign exchange student present the family with integration issues. Similarly, the return of a husband from military duty or prison or the return of a student from college involves an integration period as do smaller changes such as a spouse's assignment to a new shift at work.

A common theme seen in clinical practice, the absent-father syndrome, also involves an integration problem. In many families the father works too hard, travels too often, or drinks himself out of the picture. This situation exacerbates dysfunctional family interactions because the father is gone only temporarily; he will soon be back, and another integration period must be endured. Functionally, the returning father or the father who stops drinking creates a rift in the parenting system that can divide the family. Typically, intervention is geared to the cooperative development of house rules and structure by both parents. As the father reintegrates into the family after a long business trip or a new sobriety program, he and the mother discuss what has happened and what should be done about it after a reasonable transition period. The mother and father are thus seen as aligned and as maintaining continuity in the family's functioning. To accomplish this goal, the therapist must focus on the marital relationship, helping the couple resolve their differences. When the reason for the father's absence is pathological, this realignment process becomes increasingly difficult. After struggling to keep the family together spiritually and financially, the wife of a newly sober husband is not likely to give up control and power or even the checkbook because the risks are simply too great. Therapists must be particularly careful to benignly relabel both the old situation and the family's attempts to change. Specific change programs, too, must be carefully developed to maintain the mother's central role and the father's relatively peripheral role. One often successful technique is to reverse traditional roles: the father becomes the social-emotional spokesperson for the children, while the mother remains the final authority who establishes and enforces the rules. If the father's self-image requires that he consider himself the boss, then the father can be the rule maker but the mother monitors the children and directly administers sanctions and rewards. In either case, the mother remains the central figure.

INTEGRATING SPECIAL FAMILY STRUCTURES

With the current high rates of divorce, family therapists often encounter blended and single-parent family structures. These structures can be particularly problematic for both the therapist and the participating family members because they often involve more than one developmental phase simultaneously. In addition, these family structures often involve continuing problematic ties outside the family—to exspouses and children living with exspouses—ties that are usually close and only recently severed.

Single-Parent Families

Single-parent families are on the increase, and they now include numerous father/children families and families in which the parent has never married. However, most of the single-parent families seen in clinical practice are mother-headed groups in which the husband has left for one reason or another.

The difficulties in single parenting are numerous. Even if the mother and children are happier without the misery of a bad marriage, the mother still has a job that is often difficult for two. Roles and responsibilities, for example, can no longer be shared. Whereas in two-parent families the task-oriented parent can provide structure for young children while the understanding parent can negotiate with teenagers, the single parent must do both. Physically, too, the task is difficult. In two-parent families, one parent can be the breadwinner and the other can rear the children. If both work, they can share both tasks. The single parent must do both alone and may have insufficient time to do either; she may not have the time to effectively monitor her child or to deal effectively with an adolescent. To these difficulties must be added the numerous extrafamilial relationships that often involve stress of their own.

A therapeutic intervention that we have found useful in our clinical work indicates one way in which these difficulties can be reduced. The stress involved in parenting, providing resources, and struggling with fractured social networks increases the level of agitation within the single parent, which in turn creates a symptom of discomfort that we refer to as "the buzz." The buzz is usually strongest after a day at work when the single parent is about to go home and begin to deal with restless kids eagerly waiting for contact (see Chapter 4). Two agendas are operating here simultaneously. The single parent is looking for quiet, relaxation, and a closing down of the buzz. The kids are gearing up to engage the parent in granting requests, answering questions, and hearing complaints. As the parent opens the door, the buzz is fully developed. The single parent may signal availability out of a sense of duty yet overtly behave in a way designed to create distance (the parent may use bitchy, curt phrases, for example, or retreat to the bedroom). The kids in turn develop their own symptoms—crying, yelling, and acting up—to coerce the parent to interact with them. The parent's go-away-come-close signals create a stressful atmosphere that can become a breeding ground for chronic coercive interpersonal styles.

To remedy this situation, therapists must help single parents develop strategies that will allow them some relief yet still allow for the attention and control the children need. The single parent may, for example, be instructed to alert the children that when she comes home from work she needs 30 minutes of quiet time and that any questions from them will be answered with a "no." After 30 minutes of shared quiet time, she can see each child, one at a time, in private, to discuss requests, find out about school, and make plans. After talking with each child, she can begin normal activity such as preparing dinner and making plans for the evening. The buzz is gone, hyperactivity is controlled, and the family sidesteps the development of symptomatic behavior. The mother may even plan to go out, allowing her some independent relational payoffs.

The issue of independent relational payoffs reminds us that in some ways family therapists must learn to stop thinking in terms of single-parent families. They must recognize and incorporate into their therapeutic strategies the fact that single-parent families usually interact with other significant systems (grandparents, neighbors, opposite-sex friends of the parent) and these systems must and often can be mobilized to aid in creating effective family processes. For example, if a grandmother is attentive only when her daughter is having problems with the kids, then the therapist can see the grandmother with the family to shift her help so that it reinforces adaptive behavior instead. The male friend of a single mother can help too and in fact can be reinforced for his help. If the problems at home make the mother less able to share a positive relationship with her friend, perhaps he can help at home in return for more or even better time with the mother. The main point is that single-parent families should rarely be seen in that form. Instead, intervention should whenever possible directly involve relatives, friends, and other significant others. When seeing such groups, therapists should think about all those present in the same way they think about intact families; they should identify sequences, themes, and functions, and use techniques that will change behavior to create interpersonal payoffs for all involved.

Single-Parent Families with Two-Parent Contact

A special problem exists in single-parent families that, through divorce, still involve two-parent contact. Husbands and wives become divorced, mothers and fathers do not. In fact, they usually become grandmothers and grandfathers together. In this situation, one parent is generally responsible for the day-to-day operations of the family, while the other parent does his or her share by seeing the kids on the weekends. Mother stays home expending much effort keeping the household together, receiving little positive reinforcement for doing so, and generally feeling put upon. Father spends Sundays with the kids and in Mother's eyes reaps the benefits of her hard work. When the conflict that led to the divorce is still in operation, this problem is difficult to solve. The unresolved conflict often becomes a repository for additional conflict and family problems. The following transcript includes statements heard by countless family counselors.

Mother: I've just about had it. If Johnny doesn't straighten up, I'm going to send him back to his dad. He can raise him. . . . He can do it for a while. . . . Let him cut back on his job and his fun for a while and see how he likes it. Johnny will see that living with his dad isn't all going to the ball game and taking ski trips.

Therapist: You're still angry with your husband. What would happen if Johnny was the perfect kid?

Mother: I don't see what you mean.

Therapist: If Johnny wasn't a problem, how would you deal with your husband?

Mother: I wouldn't . . .but I have to. . . . I see him when he picks Johnny up and drops him off.

Therapist: Johnny is sort of a bridge between the two of you. Without him you may never see your husband again. Is that what you really want?

Mother: I guess so, but it's hard. I'm still close to his mother, and I still need his cooperation on certain things.

Therapist: Would you like to explore some other ways of dealing with him? After all there is still some ongoing family business which needs to be discussed.

Mother: I suppose so. It's just that I get so upset with the whole thing. I get the house, the kids, the bills, and he gets to be free and play. Johnny must think his dad walks on water. Every weekend it's some big deal. . . . Life just isn't like that.

Therapist: Johnny, do you think your dad walks on water?

Johnny: No. He does do nice things for me, but I know it's different for him. Mom thinks I don't appreciate what she does for me, but I do. Dad does what he can, but I wouldn't want to live with him. He's never home anyway.

Therapist (to Mother): Do you think your exhusband would come in here if I called and asked?

Mother: I suppose he . . . if he could fit it in.

Therapist: I'd like to meet just the two of you to see if we could clear this up a bit. Johnny, would you mind it if I met just with your mom and dad?

Johnny: No, it'd probably be a good idea.

Therapist: Good. We need to clear up what's going on so you can all get about the business of putting your lives in order.

Mother: Amen.

The solution requires Mother and Father to cooperate. Relabeling and nonblaming efforts by the therapist are critical: Father is not all-powerful; he is also lonely, frustrated, and in need of support and sometimes direction. Mother is not envious and bitchy, she too is lonely and in need of support. By cooperating and taking care of one another, the previously married people can ease the situation. Father can openly display his support and praise Mother for her hard work, and she in turn can provide him with some structure for his new role. Seeing this cooperation allows Johnny and the other children to greet Father in a relaxed fashion, thus reducing their frenetic attempts to make him feel loved and always welcome.

Blended Families

On the surface blended families may seem to be complex ones for therapists to work with. Family members have different histories, they often have difficulty in understanding or interpreting each other's motives, and once again exspouses can contribute to unwanted differences in values and behavioral styles. For the functional family therapist, however, blended families are often the easiest to work with. Because their histories are not as long as those of intact families, their behavioral styles are not as locked in and are generally easier to change. More important, the therapeutic maneuvers of relabeling and nonblaming can be easily accomplished. A stepfather, for example, can be easily excused for making mistakes because he is new to that particular situation. Teenagers who resent his presence can be legitimately relabeled as being confused, frightened, and annoyed because he is in fact an intruder. The mother, too, can be relabeled not as devious but as attempting to protect the rest of the family from mistakes that she or her new husband have made in ignorance. Children from the new marriage, rather than representing a threat to the older children, can be relabeled as a vote for family continuity. And extended families can be redefined as sources of support and new learning.

Treating the blended family requires not so much a series of new techniques as an awareness of the complexity of relationships and the sometimes strange mixture of techniques necessary to modify them. Consider for simplicity a mother, her 9- and 15-year-olds and the entering stepfather. This man must simultaneously deal with three new people and thus three new relationships, plus the various triadic arrangements. To add to the difficulty, the stepfather's relationship to the teenager is new (integrating) but must at the same time allow for the teenager's exiting process (leaving home, being more autonomous). The situation is even more complex than this, but the main thrust of the example is apparent: a mixture of styles that simultaneously facilitate integration, maintenance, and exiting (see discussions of maintenance and exiting below) must be established, and often the family cannot attain this mix. It is thus no wonder that, if problems already exist or develop, new stepfathers are willing to let the oldest child go and focus on the younger children, for whom the stepfathers feel there is still hope. The mother, however, may be less willing to do so, and this complication interferes with the marital integrating process. The therapist must recognize the developmental phases involved in each dyad and triad, help the family separate them conceptually, and initiate problem-solving styles to facilitate each. The techniques of contingency contracting and communication training, for example, can slow down the interaction pace and force family members to spend time discussing the details of their relationships, even to the point of redundancy. With blended families, these processes can be used to tease out the additional complexities that exist in this type of family.

Children in blended families can easily become caught in the middle of adult conflicts. It has been our experience that the natural parent is typically interested in working on parent/child issues, while the stepparent is far more concerned about the intimate husband/wife relationship and would just as soon not deal with the children. This mixture of agendas requires some flexibility on the part of the therapist, who must work on both areas simultaneously. An extremely important structural concept is the separation of husband/wife conflict from mother/father parenting problems. A related problem that makes blended families somewhat different from intact families is the involvement of ex-extended family members (exwives, exmothers-in-law). The problem is that an ex-mother-in-law is still a real grandmother and an exwife is still the biological mother of the children. Here again children can become vehicles for adult conflicts. This position can lead them to develop implicit control patterns (symptoms)—for example, bed wetting at the exhusband's house during his weekend with the children. The relational impact of bed wetting in many instances is to facilitate contact between the separated biological parents ("What are you doing to him that makes him so nervous?") and the bed wetting is also an expression of confusion over the sudden break in the family's stability. It is absolutely necessary in these situations to prevent adult conflict transactions from entering the children's lives and to teach both parents how to make direct statements to the children while also providing them with clear control strategies. Mothers must learn new communication techniques that will help their new husbands accept their limited role as parents during these early phases. Helping new husbands understand when to support their wives and when to take over is a critical procedure for reducing stress in the recently blended family. Working with the adults of this fractured network to give clear messages to the children and to coordinate their interactions with the children is essential.

MAINTENANCE PHASES

Most texts on family therapy, at least those that adhere to an interaction perspective, emphasize the maintenance phase in family systems. They use such terms as *status quo* and *homeostasis* to describe the relative stability of the maintenance phases. During these periods, often lasting several years, relationships remain relatively stable, and most of the interaction rules have been worked out. Relatively rigid or inflexible maintenance phases occur when the children are in the preschool and latency periods and when the family is in the latter stages of the empty nest. School and clinic referrals and divorce rates reveal that the maintenance phases are not without problems, however. For example, sibling conflict among children in the preschool and latency periods may increase. As the family attempts to gather resources to facilitate its stability and to provide a secure base for all of its members, children begin staking out territory involving these resources. Access to the television, use of bicycles, and securing parental attention are issues over which children may compete. In addition, the children are typically beginning to imitate the sex-role behaviors of their parents. Although this practice is adaptive and socially acceptable, it can present problems when the parents have not resolved certain issues about interactional rules and family roles. For example, many mothers become annoyed when their sons begin to imitate the chauvinistic behaviors of their husbands toward themselves and other women. Thus, even though it can be healthy and utilitarian, imitating sex behaviors can also produce conflict if one of the parents does not respond to that behavior in an accepting way.

In contrast to integration phases, during maintenance phases family members are usually more willing to see problems as problems. Their styles tend to be much more rigid and difficult to change, however, and the therapist often notices the absence of hopefulness, which is characteristic in newly developing relationships. In addition, attempts to change the family during these maintenance periods tend to elicit considerable resistance. Clinicians lament in particular the difficulty they encounter in securing paternal participation in working with children whose behavior is deviant.

Family Change Techniques with Preschool Children

With young children (ages 1 to 6) parents have available to them a vast array of behavior-change strategies. Because parental status is high, problems are relatively specific (tantrums, bed wetting), and the young child is comparatively receptive, strategies from the social-learning model are particularly useful. By utilizing one of the many behavior modification techniques, a therapist or parent can easily and successfully implement change programs for a variety of target behaviors. Because such excellent sources as Patterson and Gullion (1971) and Patterson (1971) are available, these techniques will not be explained here; the reader is urged to consult those sources.

In applying these techniques to young children, however, the therapist must keep in mind that success rests not with the techniques themselves but with the interpersonal transactions surrounding the target behavior. If, for example, a mother receives no reinforcement from her husband for devoting time and energy to a program that curtails their daughter's temper tantrums, the mother probably will not continue the program. The often-reported finding that parent education and training programs are not continued and do not generalize across settings (Wahler et al., 1979) attests to the importance of this issue. We have found it particularly useful for the therapist to ask two questions before instituting any parent education program: What actions do all family members take when the target behavior occurs and for 12 hours before and after? What would happen if this target behavior was not occurring? With these questions answered in terms of functional payoffs, the therapist can develop technical interventions that will produce behavior changes but also maintain these functions.

Family Change Techniques with Maturing Children

For the maturing child, the period between ages 6 and 12 is critical because during this time the groundwork for symmetrical relationships is laid. Verbal skills are adequately developed for children to begin to negotiate contracts and share feelings with their parents. However, a common mistake made by parents is to allow for negotiation in areas that are in reality not negotiable. Parents should be encouraged not to deviate from basic rules and realistic expectations. They must avoid covertly withdrawing resources and pushing children toward independence, while not being available as resources and bases of support. Otherwise, the lessening of parental contact can produce coercive behaviors in children. Thus when the natural surge toward independence begins in children, it is essential that parents increase their support (attention, structure, expectations, and consequences) and not withdraw it. Independence and autonomy can and should be facilitated but only under highly structured conditions. During this phase, an emphasis on symmetrical forms of communication (see Chapter 4) will not only facilitate independence and autonomy but set the stage for the exiting process that will follow during adolescence.

THE EXITING PHASE

Family Change Techniques with Adolescents

As children enter into adolescence (ages 13 to 18), often experiencing awkwardness, biological changes, and new feelings of autonomy and independence, so, too, do families enter a new phase of development. The relative stability and predictability of the maintenance phases tend to give way to increasing chaos. Problems with drugs, sex, parental burn-out, and adult-life change problems all face the developing adolescent. It is no wonder that understanding and acceptance are at a premium in these families. The impending adaptive departure of members of the system can be an awkward, if not traumatic, process even for some normal families because many of the rules must be changed (Haley, 1973; Hoffman, 1976). The process of homeostasis, which provided security, stability, and predictability, no longer works. A normal family is no longer a totally intact family; the rules of evolution and society dictate that the adolescent, to be normal, must begin to move toward independence and self-sufficiency. As a result, parents cannot bring things back to normal because what is normal has changed. Most families survive and some even enjoy this phase, especially when parents and children become ready for departure at roughly the same time. Family therapists, however, see families when a discrepancy exists, generally characterized by a readiness of the adolescent to move away coupled with parental unwillingness to allow or facilitate some of the changes this movement involves.

Symptoms in the adolescent's family are best understood within the context of this developmental evolution of the family. Problem adolescents can erroneously be viewed as incorrigible, truant, uncontrollable, confused, and overly influenced by peers. If, however, one views the adolescent within a relational exiting context, then it is easy to see these acting-out symptoms as operations designed to gain more distance but in ways unacceptable to other family members. Because the reinforcers available to acting-out adolescents outside of the family are so great, it is difficult to convince or even cajole them to alter their strategies. It is also difficult to change parents' perceptions of adolescents and enable them to see their children as becoming mature, especially when these children are staying out all night, missing school, or taking drugs. Parents typically increase control strategies to no avail, become frustrated, and then look to outside sources to control their teenagers. A cycle of excessive parent monitoring (merging) and increased teenage acting out (separating) is common in the families of many adolescents.

In contrast to family therapy with children, in which integration and maintenance are emphasized, treating the adolescent family requires facilitating the exiting process. Rather than developing techniques for efficient control, therapists of families with adolescents must emphasize techniques that facilitate diversity, reduced contact, and adaptive forms of independence. For example, therapists must recognize that the delinquent teenager has already initiated the process of extrafamilial movement, value differentiation, and autonomy. However, the particular ways in which the delinquent is doing so may be unacceptable to the family, the school, and legal institutions. The therapist's job is to interact with the family and other systems to help redirect the normal and appropriate developmental movement so that it is reflected in adaptive, efficient, and acceptable behavior. At the same time, the therapist must ensure that the changes also produce functional payoffs for the parents and other family members.

Thus change techniques for adolescents must not only address the eventual exiting of the adolescent but also recapture family cooperation and mutuality based now more on symmetry and less on complementarity. Negotiation and discussion combined with basic house rules must replace highly structured contingency contracting. Teenagers are no longer relatively captured, passive beings. Their emerging independence must be acknowledged, legitimized, and even facilitated. Therapists who rely on behavior modification principles must now include appropriate affective reframing in the specific change program. No longer, for example, can the therapist simply have the parents apply a contingency contracting system. The therapist must relabel the interaction as facilitating independence and demonstrating responsibility. Parental frustration must also be relabeled as continuing concern and support. With an active relabeling process and a carefully designed communication and negotiation program, adolescent autonomy and family continuity can coexist.

Family Change Techniques with Young Adults

When young adults (ages 19 to 25) are still in the home, it is always important to separate legitimate reasons for their failure to leave (economic reasons, for example) from pathological reasons. The behaviors of the late-adolescent schizophrenic function not to create freedom and independence but to encourage constraint and dependence. Until it becomes extreme, this pattern is often acceptable to parents because it extends the comfortable sameness of an earlier maintenance phase. Because the family system includes a child who has failed to develop skills that enable him or her to establish rewarding extrafamilial relationships and autonomy, intervention must focus not only on exiting but on basic skill training as well. Such intervention may take a variety of forms, including the creative yet risky emancipation or ex-communication of the schizophrenic offspring (Haley, 1973).

Techniques used during this family phase always include those that highlight individuation and increased personal autonomy for the young adult (Haley, 1980). Limitations on parental monitoring are necessary in order to legitimize the privacy and lifestyle of the young adult. In other words, such operations as developing competence builders and dealing with subsystems must shift from being a secondary focus (see Chapter 4) and instead become the major thrust of intervention. Therapists must particularly emphasize the development of extrafamilial relationships through social, vocational, athletic, and educational activities. The rest of the family must be redefined as dealing with problems of the empty nest or with marital reintegration problems. Redirecting mother/ father fights are an inevitable necessity for facilitating this retarded exiting process.

THE IMPORTANCE OF FAMILY SUBSYSTEMS

One avenue for deciding on the most appropriate target for intervention in different developmental phases is to ask this question: On a relative basis, how much emphasis should be placed on the entire system versus one or more particular subsystems? As demonstrated in previous chapters, the general functional family therapy strategy is to simultaneously deal with the entire family configuration and subsystems such as the husband/wife dyad. This overall impression of balance, however, is somewhat misleading. As children progress from infancy to adulthood, the emphasis shifts.

With young children and special structures such as the blended family, the predominant focus is on the whole family, and subsystems are conceptualized almost exclusively in the context of the entire family. When children have reached late adolescence, the family is seen less as a unit and more as a configuration of subsystems. With families of adolescents the therapist's task is to redirect the exiting struggle into a normal and appropriate developmental movement involving considerable subsystem differentiation. The family members are helped to understand and deal with the fact that they are in reality participating in two independent subsystems (husband/wife and adolescent/peers) in addition to a third intersecting subsystem (mother/father/ child). They can then learn how to interact in each of these different relationships, legitimizing each other in each relationship and learning to behave in ways that are appropriate for each relationship. Finally, in the empty-nest phase the parents and children are seen as almost separate systems that should have considerably fewer functional intertwinings than are found in families with young children.

SPECIAL FAMILY THEMES

In addition to varying in structure and developmental phase, families differ in characteristic themes and particular problem areas. These themes and problem areas tend to reflect characteristic functional relationships, and knowing what these relationships are can aid the therapist in applying the optimal therapeutic and educational techniques. In the following description, themes are grouped into one of three categories: overinvolvement, maladaptive roles, and detachment.

Overinvolvement

Schizophrenic behavior, anorexia nervosa, and sexual crimes of intimidation or aggression (including incest) are several examples of behaviors that are more than likely associated with overinvolvement themes. The overinvolvement process is easily identified in that it occupies much of the family's time and hence readily appears and reappears during intervention sessions. Overinvolvement is typified by the intense, unnecessary, and often age-inappropriate concern of one or more family members (usually one or both parents) for another family member's behavior.

Anorexia nervosa is a classic symptom of parental overinvolvement, in this case with the child's eating habits. By refusing food and incurring dramatic weight loss, the child functionally draws the parents into overinvolvement. The parents' overinvolvement, to the point of obsession, in turn functions to force the child to passively withdraw and feel resentful and angry. This cycle continues, with all members caught in a progressively provocative midpointing function of high merging behaviors coupled with powerful separating behaviors. The overinvolvement theme is also common for adolescent males who have been referred for sexually molesting young children. Typically the families of these adolescents are close, highly organized, socially isolated, and governed by intimidation strategies such as guilt, physical dominance, and threats of rejection.

Intervention with families such as these requires the often forceful blocking of the interactions that produce the unwanted behaviors. With the anorexia nervosa patient, for example, it is necessary to identify the interdependent sequences and to demonstrate that by monitoring the child's eating habits the parents are functionally facilitating the problem. The therapist must relabel their efforts as doing everything they can to help and not knowing what else to do, then shift their attention away from eating to the family's relationships, while providing another less personal and intense area of focus such as school performance. With the sexually acting out male a different kind of refocusing is often possible. The adolescent caught up in this situation is almost always involved in a meaningful hobby (usually involving digital manipulation, such as car mechanics or electronics) that is going unnoticed. Refocusing parental attention on age-appropriate issues and meaningful activities while using behavioral self-control procedures with the adolescent (often in private sessions; see Chapter 4) facilitates a modification in this overinvolvement theme that can still produce functional payoffs but not in extreme and unwanted ways.

Maladaptive Roles

During maintenance phases family members often develop maladaptive roles. A family member may take on a role that provides powerful functional payoffs and makes him or her central to continued family functioning. However, the nature of the role is such that maladaptive consequences follow for other family members.

In the *parenting child theme*, an older child carries out parental roles and responsibilities. Typically, this child has a vested interest in keeping the family focused on the trouble maker; parents use the parenting child as a snitch in order to gather information about a problem child. Another version of the parenting child theme occurs when there is a void in the parent subsystem and the parenting child is saddled with extensive child-rearing responsibilities. In many families having an older child play this role is economically and strategically necessary, but in some families it can produce adverse side effects. These pathological variations occur when the parenting child uses the role to gain immunity from adult sanction through blackmail ("I'll stop minding Jerry for you if you try and keep me in at night"). Additional difficulties arise when the parenting child role goes on for so long that the natural exiting process for the adolescent is retarded.

Related to the parenting child theme is the *good-child theme*. Functional family therapists hold that no one person is any more or less responsible for the success or pain in the family than any other person, so it follows that the good child is contributing to the dysfunction of the family on an equal basis with the "deviant" child. If we look at reinforcement schedules, we find that the good child collects an inequitable amount of positive reinforcement from parents and other social contacts because the good child is always compared with the "deviant" child. As the deviant child creates negative associations, the good child collects appropriate associations; as the deviant child becomes worse, the good child gets better. In other words, the good child has a vested interest in the continuation of deviance within the family. Any major change toward normalcy would necessitate a major change in the dispensation of positive reinforcement; thus the good child has everything to lose and nothing to gain. Intervention involves using the good child to monitor the contract and homework assignments of the deviant child for the parents. By learning new ways to maintain the reinforcement schedule, the good child can become an agent of positive change rather than the gatekeeper of the maladaptive status quo.

In the *mother-in-the-middle theme,* what started as perhaps a natural role for mother in traditional families has become dysfunctional. Mother, as the information hub, collects information about the children (school behavior, home performance, activities in the neighborhood). She then shares this information with the working father and jointly they develop parenting stategies. When this role becomes dysfunctional, the mother becomes a repository for family conflict, which remains unresolved because everything must go through her. (Readers may want to refer back to Debbie's family in Chapter 2 as an example of this theme and the strategy used to produce beneficial change.)

With all these maladaptive roles, it is critical to help the family identify adaptive role relationships (though, once again, in a non-blaming way) and to develop alternative strategies for maintaining them. In general, this process in two-parent families involves separating the mother/father conflict from other relationships. If the couple has no vehicle for resolving their conflict, it becomes diverted from the mother/father arena and thus involves one or more of the children. What was an issue between the adults ("If you really loved me you would spend more time at home") now involves the entire family ("I need you at home to help me control Jimmy's temper tantrums"). Because the wife cannot bring her husband closer, she uses guilt induction and their child's temper tantrums to functionally create this outcome. Thus Jimmy is now involved in the parents' conflict about intimacy and distance. In such a family configuration the therapist must pay special attention in the therapy phase to redefining the child's symptoms as being an expression of husband/wife relational issues. These husband/wife issues must then be dealt with therapeutically and educationally with specific techniques, after which simple educational devices to modify tantrum behavior can be instituted.

Detachment

The general category of detachment themes is the most difficult to describe. Generally, detachment themes occur in families where a decrease in membership is imminent or feared: adolescents are about to leave home; a husband or wife is considering a divorce; grandparents are considering moving to a different part of the country. In this situation, the behaviors that had produced predictable functional payoffs no longer have the desired effects. The system is changing, but since no one has yet left the family the entire system is in limbo.

Problems occur when these changes are covertly managed. For example, a couple goes to a professional for marriage therapy, but the husband is covertly seeking divorce counseling. In this case the detachment theme will quickly surface because all attempts to produce desired change will fail. The key to identifying this process is to track behavioral patterns that have recently emerged in the family. If most of these behaviors function to create distance, it is important to label this detachment process and to begin to explore its ramifications.

When detachment themes are not covert, they appear in violent and dramatic symptoms such as physical abuse and substance abuse. In these cases, family members have escalated their attempts to reverse the detachment process by keeping the family together, albeit temporarily. In the case of physical abuse, detachment is a threat because the system never successfully accomplished the integration phase. In an unsuccessfully integrated family, for example, the young child is initially controlled primarily through punishment strategies. As the child gets older and the coercive system escalates, more punishment is required, which eventually results in a battered child. Or in the case of a battered wife, her husband may once have controlled her through intimidation, but as she begins to threaten detachment the balance of distance and intimacy gained through intimidation can no longer be created. In this circumstance, the escalation to overt abuse is not uncommon.

In physical abuse cases benign relabeling is critical, although it is often difficult for therapists to accomplish. Only when both the aggressor and the victim can redefine the situation as one of functional midpointing can alternative behavioral strategies be developed. Occasionally the midpointing function can be legitimized and enhanced through the use of support groups and short periods of separation coupled with highly structured interpersonal tasks (see Chapter 4) in which the coercive cycle cannot be initiated.

In the case of substance abuse, the abuse is self- rather than other-directed. To identify the family-maintaining functions of this behavior, therapists can sometimes find clues by guessing what the family configuration would be in the absence of the symptom. For example, would the adolescent be leaving home if she did not have to remain to protect her mother from her alcoholic father? Or would the increasingly unhappy marriage relationship fragment if the parents did not have a drug-abusing adolescent to focus on?

Once again, only through focusing on all relationship patterns can particular symptomatic behaviors be put in the appropriate context and modified through educational change procedures (Haley, 1973; Stanton & Todd, 1979). Although it is important to keep in mind extrafamilial relationships with all families, in substance-abuse situations these relationships are particularly crucial. Programs such as Alcoholics Anonymous, day hospitals, and the various drug programs for teenagers provide the day-to-day support and monitoring functions that family therapists cannot provide and in addition can facilitate the vocational and social development that is so often disrupted in cases of substance abuse. Support programs for spouses such as Al-Anon are helpful (Berenson, 1976). The therapist should facilitate entry and maintenance in such programs but only in the context of intense family therapy. Without the ongoing family focus, such programs can enhance labeling the abuser as the sick one, thereby exacerbating the processes that maintained the problem in the first place (Stanton, Todd, Heard, Kirschner, Kleiman, Mowatt, Riley, Scott, & Van Deusen, 1978).

SUGGESTED READINGS

Haley, J. *Leaving home: The therapy of disturbed young people.* New York: McGraw-Hill, 1980. *This book clearly details the strategic approach to treating older adolescents and young adults. The descriptions and examples of therapeutic directives are particularly useful.*

Minuchin, S., Rosman, B. L., & Baker, L. *Psychosomatic families: Anorexia nervosa in context.* Cambridge, Mass.: Harvard University Press, 1978. *This book is the major systems-theory work on families with a psychosomatic member. The book also provides a clear description of the difference between unidirectional and systems views of behavior.*

Stanton, M. D., & Todd, T. C. Structural family therapy with drug addicts. In E. Kaufman and P. Kaufman (Eds.), *The family therapy of drug and alcohol abuse.* New York: Gardner Press, 1979. *This article provides a comprehensive evaluation of the family-systems approach to treating substance abuse. It clarifies several basic systems orientations and integrates them into a coherent treatment orientation.*

Wahler, R. G., Leske, G., & Rogers, E. S. The insular family: A deviance support system for oppositional children. In L. S. Hamerlynck (Ed.), *Behavioral systems for the developmentally disabled. 1: School and family environments.* New York: Brunner/Mazel, 1979. *This article is a ground-breaking extension of social-learning concepts to important influences that exist beyond the immediate family boundaries. The insularity concept may have as much of an impact on the maintenance of treatment effects as any single behaviorally oriented technique yet developed.*

Coding System for Therapist Skills

RATIONALE

This appendix is designed to be a training, supervision, and research tool. It describes classes of therapist behavior that have been shown to be related to the quality of the outcomes in functional family therapy (Alexander et al., 1976; Barton & Alexander, 1977; Barton & Alexander, 1980). These therapist skills are presumed to be behaviors that can be acquired. It is the presumption of neither the functional family therapy model nor the philosophy from which it is derived that these behaviors are traits.

There are two general dimensions of therapist behavior (Alexander et al., 1978): structuring skills (directiveness, clarity, and self-confidence) and relationship skills (affect/behavior integration, nonblaming, warmth, humor, and self-disclosure). The two dimensions are conceptually and statistically independent. In a general sense relationship skills are more critical for the therapy phase of functional family therapy, while structuring skills are probably more critical in the education phase. These skills are components in a host of therapeutic maneuvers; effective relabeling of clients, for example, includes clarity, nonblaming, and affect/behavior integration (Barton & Alexander, 1980). It is

Appendix A was prepared by Cole Barton, Western States Family Institute, and James F. Alexander, University of Utah.

nonetheless useful to describe and rate these skills separately. Although the behaviors can be (and usually are) confounded, they can occur in differing combinations and permutations that create different therapist styles or profiles. For example, therapists can be unclear nonblamers, just as they can be clear blamers. We have adopted the position that because there is considerable variability and there are so many differences in the total composites of therapist activity, more light is shed on therapists' effectiveness and the components of effective therapy when an effort is made to exhaustively code or rate the discrete components of therapist behavior.

Valid coding of skills requires an appreciation of the therapeutic context in which they occur. Some skills (clarity, warmth, self-disclosure) can be rated almost totally independently of the behavior of the family, while the coding of other categories requires taking into account the family's reactions (nonblaming changes the content of a family's attributions so that they are not as pejorative; humor makes someone laugh). We provide below representative examples of how each skill can be recognized by what therapists say (content), how they say it (process), and the general context of a session. Raters should attempt to code the occurrence of a skill independently of the family members' immediate reactions to it. In general, reactions to a particular skill can offer convergent validation of the impact of a particular behavior. But there is often a time lag between a therapist's maneuvers and family members' responses. A therapist may exhibit warmth for several sessions before a family responds to it, for example. The skills can therefore not be coded by family members' immediate reactions to them. Therapists may have to perform them many times before there is clear evidence that the family responds to them appropriately.

Reliability and validity issues therefore depend largely on interrater agreement. Some knowledge of therapists and an objective interrater social consensus greatly facilitate reliability and validity of the scheme. Two supervisors may recognize the subtlety in a therapist's absurd self-criticism or humor, while the family's first reaction might be that the therapist is not very bright; family members may not laugh at a joke until some of their initial anxiety has dissipated, while observers behind a one-way mirror may recognize and respond to the humor. When coding, raters should determine the presence of a skill by asking this question: For most people, most of the time, would this behavior have a high probability of eliciting the reaction specified?

CODING CATEGORIES

We will now provide specific descriptions of skills and how they are coded. We first give definitions for each of the code categories and a brief rationale for their therapeutic function. We then describe each of the skills as both a content and process phenomenon and provide global descriptions to give the reader a sense of the range of behavior that characterizes each category. These descriptions and the judgments associated with them are necessary for determining the appropriateness of a therapist's behavior in the context of a given therapy session: a therapist who is directive for 75% of an initial session will probably drive a family away, just as a therapist who is never directive will probably not engender any confidence in or respect for his or her abilities. In the section that follows this one, we describe how to array the coded therapist behavior, ways in which scores should be portrayed and interpreted, and some implications for therapist profiles.

Structuring Skills

Structuring skills are a highly interrelated set of behaviors (Alexander et al., 1976). Directiveness, clarity, and self-confidence not only create the clients' perceptions of a therapist's stereotypic professional role but are also the stylistic means by which therapists take charge and model appropriate and effective communication techniques. These skills are most obvious when therapists are trying to get their clients to do something, such as provide information, practice a technique, or create an appointment schedule. They are also obvious when a therapist must provide something for the family as an expert helper, such as expertise, modeling, or information.

Directiveness. Directiveness is usually reflected in overtly controlling behavior. Because of their one-up power position, therapists can get families to do something by being directive.

Effective directiveness can be recognized by the following behaviors:

Content (What Is Said)

Gives an instruction.
Uses imperatives and commands such as "Tell him . . . ," "Do [this] ," "Explain how. . . ."

Uses overt, nonverbal gestures to encourage more or less talking; points at someone to answer.

Process (How It's Said)

Creates compliance by family members.
Responds rapidly to messages from clients.
Presents messages as though they were nonnegotiable.

Context

Low   Avoids overt control. Won't make decisions. Can't stop family members from blaming each other. Is passive.

Generally allows family to control session. Is tentative. Pursues interpretations but backs off when opinions are challenged. Infrequently attempts to direct the flow of the session.

Moderate   Sometimes allows interaction to unfold but directs at times.

Is active. Elicits submission and questions. Changes tack if hypotheses are inappropriate.

High   Is center of interaction. Is highly verbal. Is tenacious in pursuing a topic. Won't give in.

Example of directiveness: "Turn to him and let him know how you feel."

Example of nondirectiveness: "I'm not sure what we should do now."

Clarity. Clarity is a stylistic feature of a therapist's presentations of information. It is an important determinant of how well family members understand the information presented to them and therefore of how well they are able to act on it. Because clarity is necessary to make complex information understandable, ratings should be based on a family's level of sophistication rather than on a trained professional's. ("You're covertly playing out an Oedipal theme" is elegant and clear to many professionals, but "It seems like Dad and Joey are both wanting a lot from Mom" is certainly more comprehensible and clearer to most families.)

Clarity can be recognized by the following behaviors:

Content (What Is Said)

Uses short, commonly used and understood words.
Uses short sentences.
Does not overload family with information.
Has high congruence of words and nonverbal behavior.
Uses gestures or facial expressions to amplify verbal meanings.
Gives explanations, analogies, or examples that make sense of confusing material.
Specifically operationalizes descriptions of abstract behavior.
Does not use jargon.

Process (How It's Said)

Talks succinctly, loud enough and slow enough to be heard.
Pauses for monitoring understanding or providing opportunity for questions.
Causes recipients to be attentive and to keep their comments on the same topic.
Does not cause clients to look puzzled or to have to ask lots of questions.

Context

Low   Is vague, confused, and confusing. Is unclear.

           Often mistakes or misinterprets even obvious interactions.

           Often derails. Cannot speed up interaction with observations about process, sequence, and so forth.

Moderate   Is often clear, appropriate, but can become lost if the activity is fast or complex.

           Is generally precise but occasionally overexplains.

High   Is precise, incisive, characteristically to the point. Can astutely identify sequences in a session.

Example of clarity: "When you raise your voice, your son always drops his head and stares at the floor."

Example of nonclarity: "Your family system is characterized by negative feedback."

Self-confidence. Self-confidence is important for therapists' stylistic presentations of themselves. Frank (1961) argues that therapists must present themselves as self-assured and confident to be consistent with clients' expectations and therefore to be effective. Self-confidence generally indicates competence to clients.

Self-confidence can be recognized by the following behaviors:

Content (What Is Said)

Sends optimistic messages, suggesting problems can be solved with the therapist's expertise.

Can anticipate or finish sentences others start (looks like an expert).

Makes assertive statements about the veracity, accuracy, or desirability of the therapist's presentation.

Sends messages that imply the therapist perceives self as competent.

Process (How It's Said)

Makes statements without hints of anxiety.

Presents self as expert to the family.

Reassures the family members that their problems aren't particularly difficult or unsolvable.

Is not at a loss for words; does not back off from challenges.

Context

Low	Exceptionally shy, timid, unassertive. Accepts family's limits readily even if they are contratherapeutic ("Okay, we can still meet if Dad won't come").
	Quiet, shy. Can be prodded but doesn't appear relaxed and spontaneous.
Moderate	Loses confidence when stressed but can regain it. Is variable in this regard.
	Is self-assured, confident. May lose momentum occasionally but remains confident.
High	Exudes confidence. Is almost boastful. Rarely appears tentative.

Example of self-confidence: "We're making good progress here. I'm looking forward to our next appointment. Is everyone clear on the homework assignment?"

Example of lack of self-confidence: "Will you come back even though your husband and son say they don't need this?"

Relationship Skills

Relationship skills are also a highly interrelated set but are statistically and conceptually independent from the more task-oriented structuring skills (Alexander et al., 1976). Structuring skills are relatively impersonal; they are used for getting people to do things based on the socially sanctioned status or role of the therapist. By contrast, relationship skills create a less conventional but more therapeutic, personalized relationship between therapists and clients. Research data (Alexander et al., 1976; Stuart & Lott, 1972; Weathers & Liberman, 1976) and clinical model building (Beier, 1966) show that a therapist's style of interpersonal exchange is a critical determinant of whether clients respond appropriately to later didactic or technical structuring maneuvers.

Affect/behavior integration. Such integration occurs when therapists follow a report of a behavior by identifying a feeling associated with that behavior or vice versa. Therapists may also generate both a behavioral and an affective label when family members report attributions. (Family member: "He's lazy." Therapist: "You get disappointed when he doesn't help out around the house.") When integrating affect and behavior, therapists operationalize vague reports by family members and create a cause-and-effect model for how family members feel in relation to what they do.

Affect/behavior integration can be recognized by the following behaviors:

Content (What Is Said)

Gives specific descriptions of feelings or behavior.
Explains contingencies or links between behavior and feelings—
   "When . . . , then. . . ."
Asks probing questions: "How did you feel?" "What did you do?"

Process (How It's Said)

Provides a reliable, contingent complementing of behavioral reports with affective links and vice versa; ensures that each description of a behavior includes a feeling associated with it.
Ties two or more family members' feelings or behaviors together:
   "So your . . . are related to her. . . ."

Creates a context of relatedness when people are prone to talk about feelings or behavior as occurring in a vacuum.

Context

Low   Focuses on facts presented by one person. Gives no hint that content has important affective or behavioral correlates or that other people are involved or related. Lets nonspecific information go without describing it more completely.

Has superficial reactions to feelings; gives little or no elaboration of contingencies surrounding behavior. Asks each person for his or her view without tying them together.

Moderate   Responds to reports of affect or behavior but not systematically or reliably. Tries tying things together but doesn't always establish a link.

Elicits reports of affect; amplifies family reports of affect by clarifying and pointing out contingencies. Usually complements family reports of sequences by including affective or behavioral components that are omitted.

High   Is extremely perceptive; reliably elicits and creates affective and behavioral links both within people and between people (which ties them together as a unit). Uses feelings and behavior flexibly and interchangeably to tie family members together; operationalizes vague and nonspecific information; and creates a working format for sessions.

Example of affect/behavior integration: "So when she gets really angry, you withdraw, which makes her more angry. Then both of you become afraid someone will get hurt."
Example of lack of affect/behavior integration: "So the problem is that Debbie is lazy and irresponsible."

Nonblaming. Nonblaming occurs when therapists are able to comment on family members' volatile, punitive, or punishing information without indicting any family members or accepting the veracity of a pejorative label. Nonblaming usually occurs in response to a negative comment by one family member about another. In a proactive mode, therapists must be nonblaming when probing a troublesome relationship (by not taking sides or indicting a family member) or when discussing complaints or problems (by not making issues seem dirty, sick, or evil). Blaming is extraordinarily contratherapeutic; it flies in the face of the principles of family therapies by identifying one family member as being responsible for problems. Therapists should avoid pejorative, negatively evaluative, or otherwise punishing words to ensure that no one family member is perceived more negatively than the other family members. To be nonblaming, therapists should use explanations or labels that make family members seem adaptive, reasonable, and otherwise interpersonally attractive.

Nonblaming comprises many components that are necessary and frequently occurring interpersonal reactions for effective family therapists. We recognize that there are a host of antonyms to *blaming* such as *praising* and *optimistic* that suggest, on the surface, more active therapist modes than *nonblaming, reinforcing, accepting.* Nonblaming is both more inclusive and more codeable than these styles because family members initially describe each other to therapists in punitive and punishing ways, and a host of family theorists and researchers have documented this blaming as characteristic of distressed families. Praising, optimistic, reinforcing, accepting, and other styles of this sort are therefore all subsumed under nonblaming, or are at least ways for the therapist to be in order to not blame, which is the critical process. The key clinical issue is not to respond to distressed families' characteristic blaming.

Nonblaming can be recognized by the following behaviors:

Content (What Is Said)

Uses positive or socially desirable adjectives and adverbs to describe family members.

Gives plausible explanations of family life that don't presume sickness or evil.

Makes nonjudgmental or nonevaluative comments.

Makes remarks characterized by an absence of criticism, and an absence of absolutes and imperatives: "You have to ... ," "You should. . . ."

Process (How It's Said)

Accepts and legitimizes each family member.

Diffuses responsibility by showing how all family members are related.

Points out the bright side or good news in response to the dark side or bad news.

Context

Low   Is condescending, belittling; enjoys oneupmanship. Elicits blaming, creates or maintains scapegoating. Becomes vengeful or punishing if family members oppose directions. Allows self to be drawn in to coalitions in which a third party is punished.

              Blames or judges as a vehicle for control if session is not going well or if interventions are unsuccessful. Allows members to attack each other and shows no willingness or ability to stop the process.

Moderate   Uses anger, blaming, and so forth but does so to change interaction or to change sequences in order to aid or be an advocate for the underdog. Doesn't avoid blaming but doesn't elicit it.

              Judges, blames only if pushed and tries to smooth over or cover up later. Responds to blame but does not elicit it. Has to change own meanings from bad to good.

High   Is always accepting. Effectively and reliably relabels bad as good. Is never critical. Prevents members from blaming each other.

Example of being nonblaming: "What you think is anger may be her way of expressing hurt."

Example of being blaming: "Maybe he lies because you're too strict."

Warmth. Many therapies consistently identify warmth as an important therapist skill. Warmth is also a stereotypical expectation of clients for therapists and is a generally desired attribute in helping or problem-solving situations of many kinds. Like nonblaming, warmth is presumably effective because it is not a typical reaction to the anger, apprehension of evaluation, and chaos that occur in family therapy. Warmth is communicated as much (if not more) by nonverbal as by verbal means; facial expression, posture, and tone of voice are critical components. Warmth communicates safety, acceptance, liking, support, and concern for a client's best interests and well-being. Warmth may not be reciprocated immediately by clients, so it is coded less as a contingency than are affect/behavior integration and nonblaming. The assumption is that distressed clients will take some time to begin to respond warmly either to the therapist or to each other; warmth is communicated by therapists initially as a foundation for later development in relationships. Coders should therefore develop an appreciation for whether for most people most of the time a therapist's behavior would communicate safety, acceptance, and so forth.

Warmth can be recognized by these behaviors:

Content (What Is Said)

Nonjudgmentally reflects feelings.
Communicates understanding or acceptance of a client's feelings or behavior.
Makes comments that offer support to clients.
Is not threatening or rejecting.
Expresses concern for the client's well-being.

Process (How It's Said)

Focuses on concerns of client rather than on own concerns.
Smiles, leans forward, makes eye contact.
Speaks slowly in a low, gentle voice and with sincerity.
Puts clients at ease.

Context

Low	Is cold, distant, unfriendly.
	Is businesslike. Expresses feelings only superficially.
Moderate	Is variable. Expresses warmth but can also become removed and analytical.
	Is accepting, warm. Becomes distant and analytical only if forced to.
High	Remains warm even if family is cold. Avoids pushing. Smiles often.

Example of being warm: "It is very difficult to be a parent to three kids by yourself and hold down a full-time-job. I can understand your frustration and the tears that go with it."

Example of not being warm: "When you cry like that, it makes it difficult for me to get done what needs to get done here."

Humor. The use of humor is important as another reaction to ponderous, punishing, and otherwise chaotic affect often presented in therapy. Humor can relieve tension and help family members gain a perspective on themselves. ("If this keeps up, I want a flak jacket." "How's she supposed to take you seriously if you come on like a marshmallow?") Humor can also make a therapist seem less formidable and more like a regular person, which can facilitate interaction. Humor is a contingent phenomenon that is determined by idiosyncratic tastes; a therapist who uses humor can sound hostile or be perceived as overly familiar or unprofessional. The proof of the pudding for the effective use of humor is the family's reaction to it. Therapists use humor effectively when they relieve the family's (or their own) tension, when they cast problems in a workable perspective, and when they facilitate the building of effective relationships with family members.

Humor can be recognized by the following behaviors:

Content (What Is Said)

Gives an unconventional portrayal of a situation, which lightens the mood.

Uses expressions or slang that have humorous associations for most people.

Makes things families take too seriously sound absurd.

Uses folksy analogies that capture the essence of a situation: "Sounds like you're trying to have your cake and eat it too."

Process (How It's Said)

Is accessible to the family.

Teases benevolently to draw people out.

Uses humor to cover embarrassing situations and relieve tension: "Uh-oh, I think I rattled a family skeleton."

Creates a workable situation by lightening the mood of a session.

Context

Low	Is humorless. Allows no tension release. Is always on task.
	Is not characteristically humorous. Responds to humor but never initiates it.
Moderate	Uses usual social amenities. Begins and ends sessions pleasantly. Laughs.
	Initiates humor. Occasionally turns an unpleasant sequence into a humorous one. Occasionally uses humor to identify or change a family sequence.
High	Is light, witty. Has a joking manner. Frequently turns an unpleasant sequence into a humorous one.

Example of being humorous: "Is this how you all act when you are together? If so, I'm amazed that you could get out of the house, let alone find my office."

Example of not being humorous: "I don't see what is so funny about the fights you two have. Isn't that why you are here?"

Self-disclosure. Self-disclosure by the therapist can be important both for its content and as an example of a useful process. As content, a therapist's self-disclosures can be used to introduce issues when it is clear that family members are unwilling or unable to do so ("When I feel rejected, I get very angry and I'm not very reasonable"). As this example also shows, self-disclosure can provide important modeling of a useful communication technique. The process of self-disclosure engenders reciprocal self-disclosure (Morton, Alexander, & Altman, 1976) and can therefore facilitate exchange of intimate and clinically useful information. Self-disclosure by a therapist can also communicate an egalitarian relationship between therapist and clients, facilitating personal relationships and thereby encouraging clients to remain in therapy.

Self-disclosure can be recognized by the following behaviors:

Content (What Is Said)

Makes "I" statements.
Gives examples from own experience.
Describes own feelings or behavior.

Gives reactions or hypothesizes a solution.

Gives personal feedback: "When you do that, I get a little frightened."

Gives relatively intimate personal descriptions of behavior or feelings.

Process (How It's Said)

Models effective communication skills—is personal, accepts responsibility for perceptions, feelings, actions.

Engenders reciprocol self-disclosure or is self-disclosing in response to family members' disclosures.

Promotes intimate discussion.

Is transparent nonverbally to show reactions (smiles knowingly, nods affirmatively).

Context

Low   Never discusses information from a personal standpoint; never appears to have a personal opinion; gives no reaction to information.

             Avoids personal responsibility for reports of feelings or behavior ("It seems like most people would get angry about that"). Gives a personal reaction only if family members insist.

Moderate   Demonstrates willingness to self-disclose on less intimate topics ("Yeah, I like detective novels") and occasionally gives a more personal reaction.

             Responds to family's queries with honest and intimate self-disclosure, though rarely initiates these disclosures.

High   Not only responds to the family on a personal and intimate level but reliably elicits self-disclosure from the family by initiating it.

Example of self-disclosure: "I had a difficult time when I was your age because I couldn't get my father to stop drinking. When I finally realized that nothing I did could make him start or stop, I was then able to get on with putting my own life in order. Perhaps, Debbie, your attempts to get your parents to stop fighting have kept you from getting things in order for yourself."

Example of nondisclosure: "Adolescence can be a difficult time for even the most normal family."

SCORES AND PROFILES AND THEIR MEANING

Structuring and relationship skills can be plotted as orthogonal dimensions with high and low scores on the dimensions indicating therapist performances that are associated with certain types of outcomes. Scores (the number of incidences of components of each class of skills) are plotted on a graph, with the ordinate and abscissa being the scores on relationship and structuring skills. A therapist's final categorization is determined by the point where the coordinates intersect (see Figure A-1).

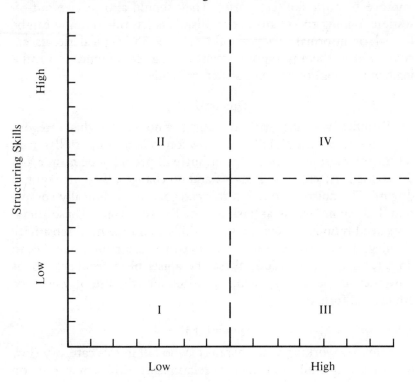

Figure A-1. Profile plot of therapist skills.

To enhance the ability to categorize therapists, each axis is divided into low and high. The intersection of the midpoints of the axes forms four quadrants. Each therapist and the family outcomes he or she usually produces fall into one of these quadrants, as described in the original research (Alexander et al., 1976). Coders should create rules for counting and creating frequency data from a role-play or therapy session, with appropriate decisions about how to sample, tally, estimate reliability, and so forth.

The following sections describe what each category means for family outcome and for the training of therapists.

Quadrant I

Families working with therapists who fall in this category (low on both structuring and relationship skills) may not come back after the initial session. Therapists who reliably fall in this category should have live supervision to provide feedback on how to improve in both skill categories. They should also receive out-of-session training to enhance relationship skills; this training can be formal or informal. They should practice the typical rituals encountered in therapy (appointment setting, communication training, contracting) to enhance structural skills as well.

Quadrant II

Families working with therapists who fall in this category (high on structuring skills and low on relationship skills) may return for more than one session but will probably be hostile and dissatisfied. After a few sessions and no changes, they may quit in disgust. Therapists who fall in this category are technically competent but come across as task-oriented automatons. These therapists need training to acquire social skills, and they need sensitivity training. They also need to learn that they can't force families to do anything. In addition, these therapists need feedback about how they come across; group feedback and the use of videotape are helpful formats.

Quadrant III

Families working with therapists who fall in this category (low in structuring skills and high in relationship skills) may stay on because they like therapy, but they don't change much and certainly not quickly. These families remain in therapy because they are nice to have around and because they still need to change. Therapists who fall in this category are enjoyable people and are liked and respected by their clients. Supervision should be aimed at getting these therapists to speed up. The therapists should work on the conceptual skills involved in assessment and in planning treatment so that they can get families to do things in sessions. The therapist should also role-play rituals like communication training and contracting. Supervisors should probe to see whether these therapists are nice and not moving because they are conflict phobic or because they can't figure out what's going on.

Quadrant IV

Families working with therapists who fall in this category (high on both structuring and relationship skills) may change quickly. Therapists in this category can flexibly perform both therapeutic and educational behaviors.

SUMMARY AND CONCLUSION

This appendix provides a framework for training and evaluating therapists. We hope that by grappling with research and methodological issues (see Alexander & Barton, 1980) we will be able to create data that empirically prove the conclusions we tentatively offer here. For now, users of this evaluation system must realize that interpretations and suggestions are based on preliminary research. Continued use of this system will, we hope, serve the best interests of clients by creating information about who good family therapists are and how to make them good.

APPENDIX B

System for Family Assessment

This appendix is designed to aid family therapists in seeking and using the assessment information that we have found most necessary and most useful. This appendix can be used as the basis for developing and planning sessions because it serves as a guide and focus for intervention. It can also be used between sessions for appraisal of both families and therapists because the format forces therapists to create information about families that can lead to therapeutic hypotheses. Finally, it can help therapists realize when gaps in information and technique do not allow a complete enough assessment for effective intervention.

CONCEPTUAL LEVELS OF ASSESSMENT

This appendix reflects the assertion that effective family therapy consists of two distinct components: therapy and education (Alexander & Barton, 1976; Barton & Alexander, 1977). Clinical intuitions about, case reports on, and experiences with family resistance argue that motivating families to change is difficult. By contrast, the social sciences provide many technologies or educational strategies to help family members actually change the form of their behavior, the degree to which they value certain emotions,

Appendix B was prepared by Cole Barton's Western States Family Institute, James F. Alexander, University of Utah, and Bruce V. Parsons, Family Therapy Institute of Laguna Beach.

and even their perceptions of the world. In short, although we have many techniques for changing family members' behavior (communication training, contingency contracting, engaging in mutual hobbies), we have been less successful in solving the more difficult problem of getting family members to perform the techniques. This appendix nevertheless does not discuss the critical therapeutic process with families. But therapists should recognize that families are not likely to respond to or adopt any educational-technological paradigms until they have been motivated to do so via therapy.

This appendix is designed to stimulate observation and analysis of the complex interplay of families and to provide functional family therapists with a format and set of labels for organizing in clinically useful ways the information they gather. Therapists working with families are most effective when they develop an appreciation of the levels of analysis crucial for assessing families and implementing change.

In order to develop this appreciation, readers should think of family assessment data as being organized on three conceptual levels: a relationship level, on which the therapist examines the interdependent properties of the family; a functional level, on which the therapist identifies the adaptive or maladaptive reliably occurring outcomes of family members' behavior; and an individual educational level, on which the therapist identifies the distinct behavioral, emotional, or cognitive changes that could be structured for and maintained by each family member. The reader will no doubt recognize the sequence of therapist activity in this organization. Until family therapists can recognize how individual behavior change can occur and be maintained in the context of the powerful influence of family *relationships* and until therapists can identify how individual behavior change can and will give personal *functional* payoffs to each family member, any efforts to force behavior change on family members are likely to be unsuccessful.

As shown in Figure B-1, therapists must develop an orderly picture of the interdependence of family members' behavior and emotions in order to identify functional payoffs for each family member. Functional family therapists must then fit the appropriate educational technology to the particular patterns that characterize the family. Until the family therapist has identified how particular educational strategies will fit the existing interdependent relationships in the family system and until the family can

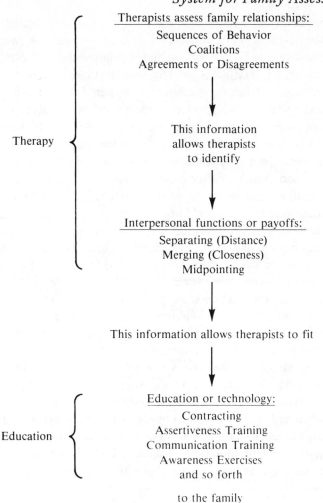

Figure B-1. Conceptual levels of assessment shown in sequence.

appreciate this fit as well, efforts to change the family will be hit or miss at best. Readers will be encouraged to find that this model does not preclude any legitimate technique for change; awareness exercises may influence styles of confrontation as readily as structured communication programs. The crucial issue is that the technology must fit the relationships and functions characteristic of the family.

Readers will be even more encouraged to find that this model of intervention does not require therapists to assume responsibility for deciding how family members should maintain their relationships or for deciding what family members should want or need. A careful and thorough assessment of relationships and payoffs reveals to the therapist what seems to maintain family members' behavior (interpersonal closeness or distance) as well as who actively initiates interaction, who mediates arguments, and other critical dimensions of relationships. The therapist can assume that the interdependence of family members and their functional pay-offs (adolescents seeking independence, wives seeking involvement from husbands) are ultimately adaptive (Klein, Barton, & Alexander, 1980). If the assessment is sufficiently inclusive, family members will seem more rational and less malevolent as a unit than they do as individuals. Other members form a benign context in which to analyze the behavior of an individual. For example, the juvenile delinquent who steals provides validity for an evil or sick label when he's rebellious and surly to his teacher or the police. This delinquent is viewed differently when it's recognized that his delinquent episodes stop Mom and Dad from fighting and get them to agree on something (even if it's what a rotten kid they have). The delinquent's surliness appears even less to be a result of craziness or malevolence when it emerges as a characteristic interaction style for all family members. Family members, if assessed correctly, present the content for both therapy ("In a funny way, his stealing seems to keep your family together") and education ("If you want your dad to spend more time with you, ask directly instead of sulking"); the therapist's problem is therefore minimized because she or he must merely fit a technology to this evidence. The therapist does not face the difficult issue of changing family members' wants, needs, or personalities but rather must fit a technology to help the family operate in efficient ways.

ASSESSMENT AS INTERVENTION
AND INTERVENTION AS ASSESSMENT

Ordinarily, assessment and intervention are considered to be distinct enterprises. But, for functional family therapists, assessment is not a passive process. At the same time that therapists are identifying how relationships operate and what functions these relationships have, they must recognize that these objective appraisals are not shared by the family and that their assessment procedures are having an impact on the family. Most of us are socialized to believe in traits, and family members are no exception. They do not share our enlightened perspective about scapegoats, identified patients, and other objective appraisals of their lives. They are typically emotionally pained and can identify only a variety of trait-oriented problems; "He's irresponsible," "He drinks too much," "She's a nag."

Functional family therapists generate the information they need in the face of family resistance and assume that family members are going to be at the least surprised if therapists do not actively cooperate in blaming, punishing, or otherwise seeing what family members consider to be the real problem. Therefore, assessment, by virtue of the content it identifies and the process through which it occurs, is in fact a powerful form of intervention. Family therapists must therefore be alert to their impact on the family. For each level of assessment, the worksheet provided at the end of this appendix lists questions or guidelines not only to help therapists objectively assess the family but to alert therapists to their impact on the family. The general form of this worksheet is summarized in Table B-1.

TABLE B-1. General form for family-assessment worksheet

		Assessment as information gathering: The family	*Assessment as intervention: My impact on the family*
Therapy	Relationships	Have I made an objective appraisal of family members?	What forms of cooperation, resistance, or change do I elicit?
		Do I see how this system works?	Have I been successful in getting family members to see the natural dependence and impact of themselves on each other?
	Functions	Can I understand why family members do what they do?	Have I been successful in getting family members to understand the adaptive outcomes of each others' behavior and to accept the legitimacy of this behavior and its nonmalevolent properties?
Education	Technology	How can I replace destructive forms with appropriate ones?	What ritual or technology have I presented effectively?

An appreciation of assessment as information gathering and assessment as intervention may help therapists identify what they need to find out, why they may find out or why they do not, and how they can help the family find out in a beneficial way. Therapists' ability to recognize not only what to focus on but how to focus on it is a crucial prerequisite for effective family change (Alexander et al., 1976).

HOW TO USE THE WORKSHEET

Therapists can use the worksheet at the end of this appendix as a check list for gathering information about families and about the therapists' impact on families. The worksheet is not intended to be comprehensive nor does it include prescriptions for doing therapy itself. Rather it guides family therapists toward information that will be sufficiently comprehensive to allow them to identify what's going on in any given family. Experience has shown that this format helps therapists to avoid the pitfalls of not being sufficiently broad and inclusive in information gathering; it helps therapists organize and integrate family information in a useful way; and it helps therapists obtain sufficient information to effectively implement a treatment plan.

A therapist will probably find the worksheet most useful if he or she reviews it between sessions to identify incomplete information about relationships in the family ("Where does Dad fit into this sequence?") and to decide what needs to be done to correct the situation ("I must include Dad more in therapy sessions and get more information about his impact on others"). The same procedure holds for considering functions for each family member, and the therapist should also be alert to how complete information at the relationship level, for example, is necessary to complete functional-level analysis ("I have found out that Dad is typically distant and uninvolved and has little contact with Mom and Suzie until a family crisis ensues; therefore, at a functional level, the arguing of Mom and Suzie serves to elicit contact from Dad"). Considering the worksheet after therapy will remind the therapist which characteristics of the family system best fit the educational plan ("Considering relationships, active Mom is probably a better candidate for initiating and monitoring behavioral contracts with Suzie than is distant, uninvolved Dad") and will remind the therapist of what will be necessary to maintain the functional payoffs of family behavior ("At the functional level, a token economy unilaterally applied by Mom and Dad will not promote Suzie's bids for independence as well as something like a behavioral contract, which she can initiate; any plan which minimizes crises must also include an opportunity for Mom to initiate closeness or contact with Dad, or she will have lost an important payoff").

FAMILY—ASSESSMENT WORKSHEET

Relationships

For assessment as information gathering, the therapist needs to understand the operation of the family as a system. For assessment as intervention, the therapist must illustrate (in a nonthreatening fashion) how each family member's behavior, feelings, and thoughts are both dependent on and necessary for those of the others. Assessment as intervention should make order out of chaos and show family members how to think about themselves and each other in different ways. A relationship focus is created by content and process, which tie family members together. It causes change because it shakes the family members' perception that the problem is a faulty individual.

Assessment as Information Gathering

What do family members spontaneously report about their own or others' feelings? attitudes? behavior?

_____

_____

Who agrees or disagrees with whom?

_____

_____

How are feelings, attitudes, and behavior assessed (good or bad) for each family member?

_____

_____

Who labels themselves as friends? Who labels themselves as combatants?

_____

_____

How do family members serve as antecedent or consequent causes of behavior?

_____

_____

Have I suggested or figured out the relationships among each family member's feelings, thoughts, and behavior?

_____

_____

Have I clarified behavioral and feeling components of attributions?

_____

_____

Have I suggested or figured out how agreements and disagreements affect everyone? Have I shown and figured out how these agreements and disagreements are not important as statements about traits but as statements about relationships?

_____

_____

Do I understand and have I included the role of the unmentioned third party in battling and supporting coalitions? Have I broadened the focus to suggest how everyone logically mediates sequences of behavior, thoughts, or feelings?

_____

_____

Have I pointed out how everybody has an impact on everybody else?

_____

_____

Have I encouraged family members to see how their feelings and behavior are related to those of other family members?

_____

_____

Functions (Interpersonal Payoffs)

For assessment as information gathering, the therapist will probably not get direct reports of the functions of behavior because family members do not think in rational or functional terms but rather in discrete, trait, cause-effect models. For assessment as intervention, the therapist should be moving toward identifying rational functions of behavior that will appear more logical and less malevolent than family members' punishing or depression-inducing explanations of behavior. At an abstract level it is necessary to understand functions to understand consistencies in behavior and what drives behavior. At a practical level, the content of functions is useful for creating effective new labels (a distancing father, for example, can be relabeled as needing to protect himself).

Assessment as Information Gathering

What kind of discrete or narrow temporal frame do family members report for meaningful family incidents and for their own behavior, feelings, or thoughts?

_____

_____

Are family members still reporting traits as initiators of sequences?

_____

_____

Are family members still characterizing each other in malevolent ways?

_____

_____

Are family members less sure than they were previously of their malevolent labels?

_____

_____

Assessment as Intervention

Have I been able to broaden the family members' discrete frame of cause-effect interpretations? Have I broadened the focus to include the whole sequence?

_____

_____

Have I been able to alert the family to the critical issue of where everyone is when the dust settles after a sequence?

_____

_____

Have I been able to understand how each family member is both a victim and a perpetrator of sequences?

_____

_____

Can I begin to give some logical and reasonable explanations for behavior, feelings, thoughts in functional terms?

_____

_____

Can I figure out and can family members begin to accept the functions or outcomes of each others' behavior and how relationships are related to these functions?

_____

_____

Education

When the therapist feels that the family is motivated and is ready to make educational changes, it is worthwhile for the therapist to consider these change efforts in light of assessment information.

Assessment as Information Gathering

Does every family member seem willing to initiate change?

_____

_____

Are family members willing to accept their own and others' functions or payoffs?

_____

_____

Do family members understand and feel comfortable with their roles in sequences and relationships?

_____

_____

Do some family members seem threatened by change?*

_____

_____

Do all family members accept themselves and others and see others in a favorable light?*

_____

_____

Are family members resisting change?*

_____

_____

---

*When the answers to these questions suggest the family won't change, therapists often question their own abilities or else blame the family. We encourage therapists to remember that it is more heuristic to assume that it's probably not that their technology is bad or that family members don't want to change. Instead, they probably need to do a more thorough functional analysis.

Do my education efforts protect family members' payoffs?

_____

_____

Does my technology capitalize on family members' values and not force them to be something they're not?

_____

_____

Am I protecting every family member's payoffs with my technology?

_____

_____

Have I made sure that some family members will not sabotage my change plans (be resistant)?

_____

_____

REFERENCES

Ackerman, N. W. Family therapy. In S. Arieti (Ed.), *American handbook of psychiatry*. New York: Basic Books, 1966.

Alexander, J. F. Defensive and supportive communications in normal and deviant families. *Journal of Consulting and Clinical Psychology*, 1973, *40*(2), 223–231.

Alexander, J. F. Behavior modification and delinquent youth. In J. C. Cull & R. E. Hardy (Eds.), *Behavior modification in rehabilitation settings*. Springfield, Ill.: Charles C. Thomas, 1974.

Alexander, J. F., & Barton, C. Behavioral systems therapy with families. In D. H. Olson (Ed.), *Treating relationships*. Lake Mills, Iowa: Graphic, 1976.

Alexander, J. F., & Barton, C. Systems-behavioral intervention with delinquent families. In J. Vincent (Ed.), *Advances in family intervention, assessment, and theory*. Greenwich, Conn.: JAI Press, 1980.

Alexander, J. F., Barton, C., Schiavo, R. S., & Parsons, B. V. Behavioral intervention with families of delinquents: Therapist characteristics and outcome. *Journal of Consulting and Clinical Psychology*, 1976, *44*(4), 656–664.

Alexander, J. F., & Parsons, B. V. Short-term behavioral intervention with delinquent families: Impact on family process and recidivism. *Journal of Abnormal Psychology*, 1973, *81*(3), 219–225.

Allyon, T., & Azrin, N. H. *The token economy: A motivational system for therapy and rehabilitation*. New York: Appleton-Century-Crofts, 1968.

179

Altman, I., & Taylor, D. A. *Social penetration: The development of interpersonal relationships.* New York: Holt, Rinehart & Winston, 1973.

Bach, G. R., & Wyden, P. *The intimate enemy.* New York: Avon, 1970.

Barton, C., & Alexander, J. F. Treatment of families with a delinquent member. In G. Harris (Ed.), *The group treatment of human problems: A source learning approach.* New York: Grune & Stratton, 1977.

Barton, C., & Alexander, J. F. Systems-behavioral family therapy. In A. S. Gurman & D. P. Kniskern (Eds.), *Handbook of family therapy.* New York: Brunner/Mazel, 1980.

Beier, E. G. *The silent language of psychotherapy.* Chicago: Aldine-Atherton, 1966.

Bell, J. E. *Family group therapy* (U. S. Public Health Service Monograph No. 64). Washington, D. C.: U. S. Government Printing Office, 1961.

Benson, H. *The relaxation response.* New York: Morrow, 1975.

Berenson, D. Alcohol and the family system. In P. J. Guerin (Ed.), *Family therapy: Theory and practice.* New York: Gardner Press, 1976.

Bertalanffy, L. von. *General systems theory: Foundation, development, applications.* New York: Braziller, 1948.

Bowen, M. The use of family therapy in clinical practice. *Comprehensive Psychiatry,* 1966, 7, 345–374.

Carson, R. C. *Interaction concepts of personality.* Chicago: Aldine-Atherton, 1969.

Coles, J. L., Alexander, J. F., & Schiavo, R. S. *A developmental model of family systems: A social-psychological approach.* Paper presented at the theory construction workshop, National Council of Family Relations, St. Louis, October 1974.

Framo, J. L. Family theory and therapy. *American Psychologist,* 1979 *34*(10), 988–992.

Frank, J. D. *Persuasion and healing.* Baltimore: Johns Hopkins University Press, 1961.

Gurman, A. S., & Kniskern, D. P. Research on marital and family therapy: Progress, prospective, and prospect. In S. L. Garfield & A. E. Bergin (Eds.), *Handbook of psychotherapy and behavior change: An empirical analysis.* New York: Wiley, 1978.

Gurman, A. S., & Kniskern, D. P. (Eds.), *Handbook of family therapy.* New York: Brunner/Mazel, 1980.

Haley, J. *Strategies of psychotherapy*. New York: Grune & Stratton, 1963.

Haley, J. An editor's farewell. *Family Process*, 1969, *8*, 149–158.

Haley, J. Family therapy: A radical change. In J. Haley (Ed.), *Changing families*, New York: Grune & Stratton, 1971.

Haley, J. *Uncommon therapy*. New York: Norton, 1973.

Haley, J. *Problem-solving therapy*. San Francisco: Jossey-Bass, 1976.

Haley, J. *Leaving home: The therapy of disturbed young people*. New York: McGraw-Hill, 1980.

Hoffman, L. Breaking the homeostatic cycle. In P. J. Guerin (Ed.), *Family therapy: Theory and practice*. New York: Gardner Press, 1976.

Jackson, D. D. The study of the family. *Family Process*, 1965, *4*, 1–20.

Johnson, S. M., & Christensen, A. Multiple criterion follow-up of behavior modification with families. *Journal of Abnormal Child Psychology*, 1975, *3*, 135–154.

Klein, N. C., Alexander, J. F. & Parsons, B. V. Impact of family systems intervention on recidivism and sibling delinquency: A model or primary prevention and program evaluation. *Journal of Consulting and Clinical Psychology*, 1977, *45*(3), 469–474.

Klein, N. C., Barton, C., & Alexander, J. F. Intervention and evaluation in family settings. In R. H. Price & P. Polester (Eds.), *Evaluation and action in the community context*. New York: Academic Press, 1980.

Lazarus, A. A. Variations in desensitization therapy. *Psychotherapy: Theory, Research, and Practice*, 1968, *5*, 50–52.

Lewin, K. *Field theory in social science*. New York: Harper & Row, 1951.

Madanes, C. Protection, paradox and pretending. *Family Process*, 1980, *19*, 73–85.

Madanes, C., & Haley, J. Dimensions of family therapy. *Journal of Nervous and Mental Disease*, 1977, *165*, 88–98.

Martin, B. Family interaction associated with child disturbance: Assessment and modification. *Psychotherapy: Theory, Research, and Practice*, 1967, *4*, 30–35.

Minuchin, S. *Families and family therapy*. Cambridge, Mass.: Harvard University Press, 1974.

Morton, T. L., Alexander, J. F., & Altman, I. Communication and relationship definition. In G. R. Miller (Ed.), *Annual reviews of communication research. 5: Interpersonal communication.* Beverly Hills: Sage Publications, 1976.

Olson, D. H. Marital and family therapy: Integrative review and critique. *Journal of Marriage and the Family,* 1970, *32,* 501–538.

Palazzoli-Selvini, M., Boscolo, L., Cecchin, G. F., & Prata, G. The treatment of children through brief therapy of their parents. *Family Process,* 1974, *13,* 429–442.

Palazzoli-Selvini, M., Boscolo, L., Cecchin, G. F., & Prata, G. A ritualized prescription in family therapy: Odd days and even days. *Journal of Marriage and Family Counseling,* 1978, *4,* 3–9.

Parsons, B. V., & Alexander, J. F. Short-term family intervention: A therapy outcome study. *Journal of Consulting and Clinical Psychology,* 1973, *41,* 195–201.

Patterson, G. R. *Families: Application of social learning to family life.* Champaign, Ill.: Research Press, 1971.

Patterson, G. R., & Gullion, M. E. *Living with children: New methods of parents and teachers* (Rev. ed.). Champaign, Ill.: Research Press, 1971.

Patterson, G. R., McNeil, S., Hawkins, N., & Phelps, R. Reprogramming the social environment. *Journal of Child Psychology and Psychiatry,* 1967, *8,* 181–195.

Patterson, G. R., & Reid, J. B. Reciprocity and coercion: Two facets of social systems. In C. Neuringer & G. L. Michael (Eds.), *Behavior modification in clinical psychology.* New York: Appleton-Century-Crofts, 1970.

Phillips, E. L. Achievement place: Token reinforcement procedures in a home-style rehabilitation setting for "pre-delinquent" boys. *Journal of Applied Behavior Analysis,* 1968, *1,* 213–223.

Rogers, C. R. *Client-centered therapy: Its current practice, implications, and theory.* Boston: Houghton Mifflin, 1951.

Rogers, C. R. The necessary and sufficient conditions of therapeutic personality change. *Journal of Consulting Psychology,* 1957, *21,* 95–103.

Rogers, C. R., & Farson, R. E. *Active listening.* Paper presented to the University of Chicago Industrial Relations Center, 1957.

Satir, V. *Conjoint family therapy* (Rev. ed.). Palo Alto, Calif.: Science and Behavior Books, 1967.

Soper, P. H., & L'Abate, L. Paradox as a therapeutic technique: A review. *International Journal of Family Counseling,* 1977, *5,* 10–21.

Stanton, M. D. Family therapy: Systems approaches. In G. P. Sholevar, R. M. Benson, & B. J. Blinder (Eds.), *Handbook of emotional disorders in children and adolescents: Medical and psychological approaches to treatment.* New York: Spectrum, 1980a.

Stanton, M. D. Strategic approaches to family therapy. In A. S. Gurman & D. P. Kniskern (Eds.), *Handbook of family therapy.* New York: Brunner/Mazel, 1980b.

Stanton, M. D., & Todd, T. C. Structural family therapy with drug addicts. In E. Kaufman & P. Kaufmann (Eds.), *The family therapy of drug and alcohol abuse.* New York: Gardner Press, 1979.

Stanton, M. D., Todd, T. C., Heard, D. B., Kirschner, S., Kleiman, J. I., Mowatt, D. T., Riley, P., Scott, S. M., & Van Deusen, J. M. Heroin addiction as a family phenomenon: A new conceptual model. *American Journal of Drug and Alcohol Abuse,* 1978, *5,* 125–150.

Stuart, R. B. Behavior contracting within the families of delinquents. *Journal of Behavior Therapy and Experimental Psychiatry,* 1971, *2*(1), 1–11.

Stuart, R. B., & Lott, L. A. Behavioral contracting with delinquents: A cautionary note. *Journal of Behavior Therapy and Experimental Psychiatry,* 1972, *3,* 161–169.

Sullivan, H. S. *Conceptions of modern psychiatry.* Washington, D.C.: William Alanson White Psychiatric Foundation, 1947.

Tharp, R. G., & Wetzel, R. J. *Behavior modification in the natural environment.* New York: Academic Press, 1969.

Tyler, L. E. *The work of the counselor* (3rd. ed.). Englewood Cliffs, N. J.: Prentice-Hall, 1969.

Wahler, R. G., Leske, G., & Rogers, E. S. The insular family: A deviance support system for oppositional children. In L. S. Hamerlynck (Ed.), *Behavioral systems for the developmentally disabled. 1: School and family environments.* New York: Brunner/Mazel, 1979.

Watzlawick, P., Beavin, J. H., & Jackson, D. D. *Pragmatics of human communication.* New York: Norton, 1967.

Watzlawick, P., Weakland, J., & Fisch, R. *Change: Principles of problem formation and problem resolution.* New York: Norton, 1974.

Weakland, J. H. Communication theory and clinical change. In P. J. Guerin (Ed.), *Family therapy: Theory and practice.* New York: Gardner Press, 1976.

Weakland, J. H., Fisch, R., Watzlawick, P., & Bodin, A. M. Brief therapy: Focused problem resolution. *Family Process,* 1974, *13,* 141–168.

Weathers, L., & Liberman, R. P. Contingency contracting with families of delinquents and adolescents. In C. M. Franks & G. T. Wilson (Eds.), *Annual review of behavior therapy: Theory and practice* (Vol. 4). New York: Brunner/Mazel, 1976.

Wood, P., & Schwartz, B. *How to get your children to do what you want them to do.* Englewood Cliffs, N. J.: Prentice-Hall, 1977.

Zuk, G. H. Value conflict in today's family. *Marriage and Family Living,* 1978, *60,* 18–20.

Index